Native American Mythology

Q. L. PEARCE

LUCENT BOOKS

A part of Gale, Cengage Learning

GALE
CENGAGE Learning·

Detroit • New York • San Francisco • New Haven, Conn • Waterville, Maine • London

LIBRARY OF CONGRESS CATALOGING-IN-PUBLICATION DATA

Pearce, Q. L. (Querida Lee)
  Native American mythology / by Q. L. Pearce.
    p. cm. -- (Mythology and culture worldwide)
  Includes bibliographical references and index.
  ISBN 978-1-4205-0716-4 (hardcover)
  1. Indian mythology--North America. I. Title.
  E98.R3P44 2012
  398.208997--dc23
<div align="right">2011052630</div>

Lucent Books
27500 Drake Rd.
Farmington Hills, MI 48331

ISBN-13: 978-1-4205-0716-4
ISBN-10: 1-4205-0716-8

Printed in the United States of America
1 2 3 4 5 6 7 16 15 14 13 12

TABLE OF CONTENTS

Native American Tribal Regions

Subarctic

Arctic

Pacific
Northwest
Coast

Plateau

Northeast

Great
Basin

Great
Plains

California

Southwest

Southeast

Mesoamerica

Caribbean

Arctic

Aleut
Inuit
Inupiaq
Yup'ik

Subarctic

Anishinabe
(Chippewa,
Northern Ojibwa)
Carrier
Chipewyan
Chilcotin
Cree
Dogrib
Han
Hare
Holikachuk
Kaska (Nahane)
Koyukon
Kutchin
Mountain
Naskapi
Sekani
Slavey
Tahltan
Tanacross
Tanaina
Tasttine (Beaver)
Yellowknife

Northwest Coastal

Bella Bella
Bella Coola
Chinook
Clatsop
Clatskanie
Comox
Eyak
Haida
Kwakiutl
Musqueam
Nanaimo
Niskwalli
Quileute
Samish
Sauk
Skagit
Snohomish
Sooke
Tillamook
Tlingit
Tsimshian
Yaquina

California

Achomawi (Pit
River Indians)
Bear River
Chauilla
Campo
Chukchansi
Chumash
Chilula
Chimariko
Costanoan
Hupa
Ipai
Karok
Klamath
Luiseño
Maidu
Migueleño
Miwok
Monache
Nakipa

Pomo
Quechan
Rumsen
Salinan
Santa Catalina
Serrano
Shasta
Tipai
Tolowa
Tongva
(Gabrielino)
Wappo
Wintun
Yana
Yaqui
Yokuts
Yurok

Plains	Northeast Woodlands	Southeast Woodlands	Southwest
Arapaho	Abenaki	Ais	Acoma
Arikara	Algonquian	Alabama	Apache
Assiniboine	Anishinabi	Apalachee	Cocopa
Blackfoot	(Chippewa/Ojibwa)	Atakapa	Havasupai
Brule	Beothuk	Biloxi	Hohokam
Caddo	Erie	Caddo	Hopi
Cheyenne	Fox	Calusa	Jumano
Chickasaw	Ho-Chunk	Catawbe	Karankawa
Comanche	Huron	Cherokee	Keres
Crow	Illinois	Chickamauga	Laguna
Gros Ventre	Iroquois	Chickasaw	Los Luceros
Hidatsa	Cayuga	Chitimacha	Maricopa
Iowa	Mohawk	Choctaw	Mohave
Kaw	Oneida	Creek	Nambe
Kiowa	Onondaga	Hitchiti	Navaho
Lakota	Seneca	Lumbee	Pecos
Mandan	Tuscarora	Mobile	Pima
Missouri	Kickapoo	Natchez	Pueblo
Osage	Laurentian	Pensacola	Quechan
Ottawa	Maliseet	Seminole	Seri
Pawnee	Mascouten	Timucua	Taos
Ponca	Massachusett	Tuskegee	Tewa
Quapaw	Menominee	Tutelo	Tohono
Sioux	Miami	Tunica	Walapai
Sauk	Micmac	Yamasee	Yavapai
Tonkawa	Mahican	Yuchi	Yuma
Wichita	Mohegan		Zuni
	Nanticoke		
	Narragansett		
Great Basin	Neutral	**Plateau**	
	Ottawa		
Bannock	Passamaquoddy	Cayuse	Nicola
Gosiute	Penobscot	Coeur d'Alene	Okanagan
Kawaiisu	Pequot	Flatbow	Palus (Palouse)
Mono	Potawatomi	Flathead	Rock Creek
Paiute	Powhatan	Fountain	Sanpoil
Panamint	Sauk	Kalispel	Shuswap
Paviotso	Shawnee	Kittitas	Spokane
Shoshone	Susquahannock	Klamath	Thomson
Timbisha	Wampanoag	Kootenai	Umatilla
Ute	Wappiger	Lillooet	Walla Walla
Washo	Winnebago	Modoc	Yakima
		Nez Percé	

Major Characters in Native American Mythology

Character Name	Pronunciation	Description
Arrow Boy		Cheyenne cultural hero
Awonawillona	AWN-nah-wee-yona	Zuni creator deity
Begochiddy	BEY-go-chid-dee	Navajo creator deity
Born for Water		Navajo twin son of Changing Woman
Changing Woman		Navajo Earth mother and creator
Coyote		Multiple tribes, trickster
Fire Beings		Karok fire spirits
First Man		Multiple tribes, first male human
First Woman		Multiple tribes, first female human
Fire God		Navajo fire deity
Glooskap	KLUE-skopp or GLOOS-kahb	Northeast Woodlands culture hero
Hahskwahot	HAHS-kwa-hot	Iroquois storyteller spirit
Holy People		Navajo Spiritual beings
Hutash	OO-tach	Chumash creator deity
Inyan	EEN-yahn	Lakota rock deity
Kachina	kuh-CHEE-nuh	Hopi spirit figure
Kloskurbeh	CLOSE kur beh	Penobscot all maker/creator
Maka		Algonquian spirit
Manitou	MAN-ih-TOO	Lakota Earth deity
Massau	MAH-soo	Hopi Kachina Earth guardian
Monster Slayer		Navajo twin son of Changing Woman
Mother Corn		Penobscot First Mother
Ocasta	oh-kus-tuh	Cherokee god of knowledge
Old Man		Blackfoot culture hero and trickster
Olelbis	o-LEL-bay	Wintun creator god
Qalupalik	Kah-loo-pah-lik	Inuit evil sea spirits
Salt Woman		Zuni, Navajo creator of salt beds
Sedit	se-DEET	Wintun antagonist of Olelbis
Sedna	SED-nuh	Inuit mother of the Oceans
Selu	SHELL-oo or SAY-loo	Cherokee Corn Mother
Sky Woman		Iroquois First Mother
Spider Woman		Navajo creator deity

Character Name	Pronunciation	Description
Tabaldak	TAH-bal-daak	Abenaki creator deity
Tawa	tah-wah	Hopi creator sun deity
Three Sisters		Multiple tribes, divine incarnations of corn, beans, squash
Tirawa	TEER-un-wuh	Pawnee creator deity
Wakan Tanka	Wak-un TAN-kuh	Lakota creator deity
White Buffalo Woman		Lakota cultural deity
Windigo (or Wendigo)	WHEN-dee-go	Algonquian cannibal monster
Yundi Tsundi	YOON-dee SOON-dee	Cherokee nature spirits

The Nature of Myth

Mythology is a complete body or collection of ancient stories associated with a group of people with a shared culture. To a modern audience the characters and events of myths may seem unusual, but the storytellers of long ago viewed the world differently than people do today. They interpreted events on the basis of their knowledge and experiences, and they often used symbolism to make a point. In their *Handbook of Native American Mythology,* authors Dawn E. Bastian and Judy K. Mitchell remark that myths are "true because they are based on reality and address issues of the tangible world in which we live, even if the characters and events themselves are imaginary."[1] Whether a myth is historically factual is less important than the meaning of the story to its people. The collected myths of a society are a window on that society's cultural identity, including its history, values, customs, and beliefs. Researchers note that "in societies where myth is still alive the Natives carefully distinguish myths, 'true stories,' from fable or tales, which they call 'false stories.'"[2]

Around the world, myths have been handed down from generation to generation to explain, teach, guide, inspire, or even to entertain. In many cultures, such as those of ancient

Greece, Egypt, and Japan, myths are usually written, but American Indian storytellers and spiritual leaders preserved their mythology through a rich oral tradition. Native American myths were originally told in order to explain such things as how the universe began, how everything in it came to exist, where people came from, and how the natural world worked. The stories often involved supernatural beings, animals, or magical events.

The spirituality, mythology, and everyday life of North America's First Peoples was intricately linked to the land and its rhythms. The mythology of Native Americans helped them to survive and flourish in their environment because the stories contained lessons on proper behavior and how to carry out everyday tasks from building a shelter to preparing a meal. They also explained why and how people were to perform important rituals. Anthropologist Bronislaw Malinowski wrote of the role of myth in human society, "Myth is thus a vital ingredient of human civilization; it is not an idle tale, but a hard-worked active force; it is not an intellectual explanation or an artistic imagery, but a pragmatic charter of primitive faith and moral wisdom."[3] Native Americans of today who follow the traditional spirituality of their ancestors continue to describe these myths as a very important part of their culture.

When exploring the mythology of North America it is important to note that the term "Native American" is used to describe hundreds of different tribes that occupied the continent before the arrival of Europeans in the fifteenth century. Similarly, the mythology of North America varies from one region to another. While no single body of myths is shared among all of the tribes, many similarities can be found in the overall themes and characters. Myths also highlight the similarities and differences among tribal groups.

Native American myths reflect the unique perception of American Indians, which is based on their experience. Some of the connections and deeper meanings in the stories might be difficult for people from other cultures to understand. The stories must be viewed respectfully and with an open mind. The opportunity to hear a tale told by a Native

American storyteller can be a remarkable experience that helps to put a myth into the proper perspective. As the hundreds of Native American myths were told through the centuries, they have changed in the telling, so many variations of the same myths have appeared. The best way to study native myths is to put them in context by learning about the cultures that produced the stories.

CHAPTER 1

The First Peoples of North America

Native Americans have lived in North America for thousands of years. The archeological record about the earliest Native Americans or Paleo-Indians is incomplete. Most archaeologists suggest that they migrated from Asia, but when and how that happened is a topic of debate. It is likely that small groups of hunter-gatherers arrived between eleven thousand and eighteen thousand years ago, though there is some evidence that it could have been as long as thirty thousand years ago or more and that migration may have taken place in several waves.

During the last Ice Age, when the planet was much colder, migration was made possible by the unique environmental conditions. The earth regularly experiences cycles, called glacial periods, which span many thousands of years. During these periods the planet's ice sheets advance and retreat. About twenty thousand years ago ice sheets covered much of the North American continent. So much ocean water was frozen into the ice that sea levels were much lower than they are today. Land that was usually under water was exposed. For example, the Bering Strait, a narrow body of water between what is now Russia and Alaska, may have been a string of islands or a dry land bridge. It may have become a migration route for Ice Age mammals that were followed by human hunters. As the climate warmed and the ice retreated, sea levels rose, and the land bridge disappeared. In addition to a land bridge, archaeologists suggest that some early people may have arrived in North America by boat, then traveled along the Pacific coast into Alaska and Canada.

There is evidence that the Paleo-Indians had stone tools and weapons, fire, and knowledge of medicinal plants and that they were skilled at such things as making nets, basket weaving, and more. The new world that the First Peoples found covered more than 7.6 million square miles (19.7 million sq. km), and it included every type of environment from frigid arctic tundra to warm, wet subtropical swamps, dry deserts, dense forests, grasslands, shorelines, river basins, and mountains. Over several thousands of years groups settled in different areas and developed specific skills that helped them to adapt to their surroundings. In environments with mild weather and good soil some groups developed farming practices and built permanent villages. When Europeans arrived in the fifteenth century, North America was home to several million people divided into hundreds of tribes with distinct languages and traditions, including rich, dynamic mythological traditions. The stories and characters in the myths reflected the environmental pressures, social structures, and spiritual beliefs of the cultures that created them.

Hunters follow animals across a land bridge that may have existed between what is now Russia and Alaska more than twenty thousand years ago. Some archeologists believe that the first people to migrate to the North American continent arrived via this route.

A Different World

The Earth looked different eighteen thousand years ago. The worldwide sea level was about 400 feet (120m) lower. Ice sheets as much as 2.5 miles (4km) thick covered what is now Canada, the Great Lakes region, and New England. In Europe, Scandinavia and the United Kingdom were under ice.

There is no single Native American mythology, but stories told by groups with comparable lifestyles share some universal themes and have many similarities. Historians generally divide the tribes that represent the ancestry of modern Native Americans into ten geographical regions with flexible borders. These regions create a framework for putting the myths into context. One of the most challenging regions for survival was that of the frigid Arctic.

The Far North

The Arctic region of North America, which included the northernmost coastlines of what is now Alaska and Canada, was home to tribes such as the Aleut, Yupik, and Inuit, who shared many social and spiritual characteristics. Long, dark winters and short, wet summers made the treeless tundra unusable for farming, so the people developed a hunter-gatherer culture. In some places they foraged for wild berries, roots, and grasses, but hunting was the main source of food. The sea offered fish, seals, walrus, whales, and shorebirds. Herds of caribou wandered across the land. The animals provided more than meat. Their hides, fur, bones, feathers, and teeth were used for clothing, tools, utensils, weapons, and building materials. The Aleut and Yupik lived mainly in permanent villages. Using materials such as driftwood, sod, whalebone, and animal skins, they built houses that were occupied by several related families who shared the communal living space. The Inuit of central Canada were nomadic. Traveling overland on foot or by sled, they followed the food sources and lived in portable dwellings made of seal or walrus hide. In winter they sometimes built temporary shelters with blocks of snow.

Arctic peoples relied on the ocean for survival, and their mythology was greatly influenced by the sea, animals, and hunting. They believed that animals could shape-shift into human form and had "the magical power to hear and understand the human word. For this reason, hunters in their camps, when singing or speaking of walrus or seal, may carefully refer to them as maggots or lice, or call caribou lemmings, thus confusing the animals that are necessary for their survival,"[4] according to author James Houston.

Life for Arctic tribes was difficult and dangerous, so their myths often reflected the perils of their harsh environment. The myth of the Qalupalik was a frightening story that kept children from playing on hazardous sea ice. The

Inuit hunters stalk walrus near dangerous icy waters. Native people of the Arctic told children a myth about frightening sea creatures called Qalupalik to keep them from venturing too close to broken ice.

Qalupalik were ocean creatures with a human form; green, scaly skin; long hair; and long, sharp fingernails. They would lurk near patches of broken ice waiting to snatch children who wandered too close to the water. According to the myth, waves of steam rising from the water were signs that a Qalupalik may be just below the surface. Elders claimed that the creatures would hum eerily or knock on the ice beneath a potential victim's feet. Stolen children were said to be stuffed into a pouch and pulled under the water, never to be seen again. By encouraging children to be cautious, the myth contributed to keeping them safe in a harsh environment.

The boundary between Arctic and subarctic was marked by a change from treeless tundra to forests of aspen, birch, and pine. The land was dotted with mountains, prairies, and many lakes and rivers. As many as thirty different tribes, such as the Anishinabe, Ingalik, Hare, Chipewyan, and Cree, lived in the huge, sparsely populated region. The people gathered edible plants when they were in season, and the forests were filled with big game such as moose, deer, and elk and small animals such as beavers and muskrats. Even though food, furs, and skins were available, the climate was harsh, and hunting could be difficult during the heavy summer rains or in the deep, freezing snows of winter. The people were nomadic, and they traveled by foot, birch bark canoe, or, in winter, by toboggan or snowshoes. They were organized in local bands made up of extended families that lived in a variety of structures such as plank houses, pit houses, or skin- or brush-covered domes. Since their survival depended on the creatures they hunted, subarctic cultures viewed animal spirits as a source of power, and some myths described animals as the original inhabitants of the earth. Like that of the Arctic, subarctic mythology included stories that warned about what would happen if people acted recklessly or disobeyed bans the tribe placed on certain behaviors. For example, a starving person who ate human flesh, which was forbidden, could be possessed by the spirit of a Windigo (sometimes spelled Wendigo). Tribal elders told many frightening stories about the mythological monster that lived in the forest and preyed

CAHOKIA

The Art Institute of Chicago had an exhibition in 2004 and 2005 called *Hero, Hawk, and Open Hand: American Indian Art of the Ancient Midwest and South*. It was named for three motifs, or designs, that represent life, death, and renewal and are often found in native mythology. Some of the earliest examples of these motifs are from Mound Builder societies in the midwestern and southern United States. Between fifteen hundred and eight hundred years ago these complex societies led by chiefs built pyramid mounds, adopted agriculture, established settlements and major cultural centers, and engaged in trade with similar settlements. Evidence of such places has been found in Ohio, Indiana, Illinois, and other states. One of the main sites is called Cahokia (kah HOE kee uh). It was a great ceremonial center built near where the Missouri, Ohio, and Illinois Rivers meet the Mississippi. During its prime in the fourteenth century, Cahokia was home to as many twenty thousand people. At its center was a huge human-made earth mound 100 feet (30.5m) high. Surrounding it were acres of commercial and residential areas as well as fields where corn and other crops were raised. Cahokia was a center for ceremony and the arts. The objects exhibited at the Art Institute of Chicago demonstrated that mythology was an important element of the culture of Cahokia. The exhibit included ceremonial pipes carved in animal forms, as well as shells, copper plates, ceramics, and stone figures engraved with mythic symbols and images of heroes and supernatural characters. The art produced at Cahokia spread to other areas and reinforced the myths it depicted. Researchers think that in the fifteenth century, drought, crop failures, deforestation, and overhunting by the huge populations caused people to leave the city. European contact and exposure to disease may have contributed to the final collapse of Cahokia.

The Cahokia Mounds in Illinois, site of a large native city in the fourteenth century, are visited by tourists today.

on humans. Subarctic mythology was also filled with tales of tricksters and shape-shifters. They shared many of these beliefs with people of the Northwest coastal region, which curved along the western coast of the continent.

The West Coast Regions

Unlike their northern neighbors, the Northwest coastal tribes such as the Tlingit, Haida, Coast Salish, and Chinook enjoyed a fairly mild climate. The warm Japanese Current flowed through the ocean waters to the west, and the mountains blocked colder air from the east. Though groups moved to follow seasonal food sources, many lived in winter villages of one hundred or more related people with a complex social structure led by a chief. Large villages had thirty or forty rectangular cedar-plank houses arranged in rows. The front of each home was usually painted with clan symbols and images of mythical beings. Some sported huge totem poles that represented the story of each clan. The rich coastal culture was supported by plentiful natural resources. Forests of fir, cedar, and spruce trees covered the mountains and provided wood, bark, and fiber for homes, canoes, clothing, baskets, and blankets. A wide variety of wild plants supplied food and medicines, while game animals such as deer, elk, moose, mountain goats, fox, and beaver were the source of

Pomo people gather acorns, an important food source for many traditional California tribes.

meat and fur. The native peoples were skilled at hunting and fishing, and their diet included whale, seal, sea otter, and many species of fish caught with cedar nets, traps, and spears.

The myths of the Northwest coastal tribes often outlined respectful ways to treat the animals they hunted and fished for. For example, early people believed that salmon lived on the ocean floor in houses. Each season a single salmon swam up and allowed itself to be caught. If people honored its sacrifice by cooking it according to ritual, sharing it with everyone, and returning the bones to the water, the fish would return to life. It would then swim to its home and tell other salmon that it had been treated respectfully. This guaranteed a good fishing season. The regional mythology also focused on important landmarks. Mount Rainier, the highest peak in the Cascade Range, is named in a myth of a great flood as the place where survivors took refuge from the rising water. The native name of Mount Rainier varied by tribe, but the Chinook nation name of Tahoma was well known.

Like their north coast neighbors, the Native Americans of California were fortunate to live in a favorable environment. From north to south there was a great diversity of language and climate, but there were many cultural similarities as well. The northern and central areas of the region included tribes such as the Shasta, Karok, Yurok, Hupa, and Miwoc, who established villages along the coastlines, lakeshores, and riverbanks of their lands. The canoe was a common mode of travel. Forests of giant redwood trees were home to deer, and the trees provided material for boats, houses, clothing, and tools. Oaks offered acorns, an important food source that could be stored for long periods. People also ate salmon, turtles, and eels. The eastern part of the region was high desert where deer, rabbit, seeds, berries, and tubers were typical fare. Regional mythology was often localized and included origin and creation tales as well as stories of heroes.

The environment of the southern part of the region varied from coastal wetlands in the west to the deserts in the east. It was home to people of the Serrano, Gabrielino (Tongva), and Cahuilla tribes, among others. The inhabitants took advantage of the resources that were available. Those who lived near the shore depended on fish and shellfish, while desert dwellers relied on rabbits and deer, as well as acorns, seeds, and native grasses. Origin, animal, and trickster myths were common in the area. A unique origin myth was that of the Chumash, who lived on the mainland and on the islands just off the coast.

According to the story, the Earth deity Hutash created the first Chumash people on Santa Cruz Island. They multiplied quickly and soon outgrew the island. Hutash decided to help some of the Chumash to reach the mainland, so she created a rainbow bridge from the island to the coast. A few of those who crossed slipped from the bridge and fell into the ocean. Hutash did not want them to drown, so she turned them into dolphins. To this day the Chumash honor dolphins as their brothers. Animal and origin myths were also popular with groups that populated the Columbia Plateau to the north of California and the Great Basin regions to the east.

The High and the Low

Two regions occupy the highlands of the Columbia Plateau and the lowlands of the Great Basin that make up the land-locked area between the Rocky Mountains and the Cascades. The plateau cultures included the Nez Percé, Spokane, Yakima, Klamath, and Modoc. Like most other Native Americans of the time, they structured their lives around the seasons and the availability of food. The Rocky Mountains on the east and the Cascade Range on the west formed natural boundaries, and the interior was a patchwork of forests and grasslands that were a source of wild roots, berries, pine nuts, sunflower seeds, and the starchy bulb of the camas, a type of lily. The people hunted wild game such as rabbits, deer, elk, and mountain sheep. In general they lived as peaceful bands in small villages along the banks of rivers such as the Columbia, the Fraser, and their tributaries. This enabled them to travel and conduct trade. Small family groups wintered in circular log homes built partly underground to avoid temperature extremes. In summer they built light dwellings with cottonwood frames covered in mats woven from bulrushes that grew in the shallows of the rivers.

Many plateau myths are about landmarks such as Mount St. Helens, Mount Hood, and Crater Lake. One of the most popular characters of the region is Coyote. The mythology of the Nez Percé includes a unique creation story that features the trickster. The story takes place before the creation of humans at a time when all of the animals of the plateau lived together as friends. One day a gigantic monster arrived and began to devour animals by sucking them in with its powerful breath. When Coyote returned from a journey he realized that many of his friends were missing. When he saw that the monster was swallowing them, Coyote was angry, but he was also smart. He quickly came up with a plan to save his friends. He swam across the Snake River and tied himself to the three highest mountain peaks with a strong rawhide rope. Once he was ready he called out and challenged the monster to eat him. The monster laughed and sucked in the air all around Coyote, but the trickster did not move. After several tries the monster gave up. Thinking that

A Native American fishing camp sits on the banks of the Columbia River in the Pacific Northwest.

Coyote may have magical powers, he proposed they call a truce and become friends. At first Coyote pretended to agree, then he tricked the monster into showing him the inside of its stomach. Once inside, Coyote found his friends. Working quickly he killed the monster by cutting out its heart. As soon as the animals were safely outside, Coyote sliced the monster into pieces, which he tossed all over the land. Wherever the pieces landed they became a nation of people, including the Cayuse and Yakima. As Coyote washed the monster's blood from his hands, the drops became the people of the Nez Percé tribe. "They will be few in number, but they will be strong and pure,"[5] Coyote announced. And that was how the human beings came to be.

The Great Basin lies south of the Columbia Plateau. It was named for the low desert and salt flats that stretched between the southern Cascades, the Sierra Nevada, and the Rocky Mountains. The region covers an area where temperatures could rise to 100°F (37.7°C) in summer and drop below -20°F (-29°C) in winter. The scattered population included Ute, Shoshone, Washo, and Paiute people. There was little regular rainfall, so farming was not common. Large game animals such as pronghorn antelope and deer were scarce. During the summer, people ate hares, snakes, insects, lizards, wild seeds, roots, berries, and cactus fruits, some of which they preserved and stored for winter.

The Great Basin tribes each spoke one of six related languages. Some groups were nomadic, traveling in family bands led by an elder. They built simple shelters from willow poles covered with reeds or brush then abandoned them when they moved on. Those who lived on lakeshores or near marshes built larger, more permanent camps. Large groups gathered at certain times of the year for ceremonies or harvests. The wild piñon nut was a very important food in the region, and the piñon harvest was a time of ceremonies and celebrations. The lowland piñon forests were considered sacred. Many people met there in fall for the first fruit celebrations to harvest the nuts and show respect for the forests.

The mythology of the Great Basin highlighted mythical animals, such as Wolf, Coyote, Rabbit, Bear, and Mountain Lion, that could speak and behave much like humans. The animals were credited with creating food resources, seasons of the year, and much more. Heroine and trickster myths were common in the Great Basin and also on the Great Plains beyond the Rocky Mountains to the east.

From the Plains to the Desert

The Great Plains was an enormous grassland that dominated the center of the North American continent from the Rocky Mountains to the Mississippi River. To non-Indians, some of the most recognizable names of Native American tribes are those of the Great Plains region: Crow, Sioux, Cheyenne, Arapaho, Osage, Kiowa, and more. For at least two centuries the image non-Indians had of Native Americans was based on what they knew about those tribes, but much of what they knew was incorrect. Considering the thousands of years that Native Americans have lived in North America, the legendary image of the Plains Indian on horseback is a comparatively new one.

The Great Plains region is a land of change, and it has been home to many cultures. Groups such as the Mandan, Iowa, and Missouri peoples lived in villages of temperature-efficient earth-covered lodges along lakeshores and riverbanks. They had a complex clan-based social structure. Councils representing each clan led villages, which often joined together in confederations. Seasonally the men would hunt for buffalo, deer, and wild turkeys, but additional food came from their own fields of corn, beans, squash, melons, sunflowers, and pumpkins.

The farming cultures shared the Great Plains with many other tribes, such as the Cheyenne, that had migrated from other areas, often led by chiefs with recognized hunting skills. Until the middle of the nineteenth century, millions of buffalo gathered in massive herds across the grasslands. Plains people not only ate buffalo meat but used the fat for cooking,

A Native American hunts buffalo on the Great Plains. The prominence of buffalo in the mythology of Great Plains tribes reflects the animal's importance to their way of life.

hides for clothing and shelter, and bones and horns for tools. Even the tails were used as fly swatters. The mythology of the Great Plains included dozens of myths related to these animals. Many Cheyenne avoided eating buffalo meat that came from just under the animal's throat, and one of their myths explains why. According to the story, buffalo once hunted and ate humans. The tables were turned when the buffalo lost a bet on a race between humans and animals. Knowing that humans would soon start hunting them, the buffalo told their children to hide and to store the last of their human flesh in a skin pouch on front of their chests. The Cheyenne did not consume the throat of the buffalo because the myth suggested that it might be made from human flesh.

At its southern tip the Great Plains share a border with the Southwest region. Archaeological evidence suggests that parts of the Southwest region have been occupied for at least six thousand years. At first the people who lived there hunted deer, antelope, and rabbits and gathered wild food such as yucca and prickly pear. Around thirty-five hundred years ago they began to grow maize (corn), squash, beans, and other crops. The people developed sophisticated irrigation systems to enable the crops to survive in the dry climate.

Many of the tribes that later occupied the region were also excellent farmers, including the Hopi, Zuni, Mojave, Pima, and Navajo. The Hopi and Zuni raised maize, squash, and beans, and they later raised cotton and were expert weavers. They lived in communal buildings made of adobe brick. The buildings were stacked one on top of the other like an apartment complex.

Emergence stories are an important element of their mythology. In emergence myths people are created in a level deep within Earth, and they travel up layer by layer until they emerge to make their home on the planet's surface.

Similar to the Great Plains region, the Southwest farming cultures shared the land with nomadic hunters who migrated into the area. These included the Yavapai and the Apache. The Apache Nation was made up of many distinct smaller groups such as the Chiricahua, the Jicarilla, and the Mescalero, and they were closely related to the Navajo. Their homes were brush huts called wickiups, and they lived in family bands led by a chief chosen in part for being hard working, generous, and fair. The mythology of the different Apache groups varies, but cultural heroes and tricksters were typical characters.

To the Eastern Shores

The people of the Northeast woodlands represented a variety of rich cultures, often grouped by the language they spoke. Algonquian speakers included the Micmac, Abenaki, Ojibwa, and Fox. Iroquoian speakers were Seneca, Mohawk, Oneida, and Huron, and Siouan speakers included the Winnebago.

The environment of the Northeast was varied. Spruce, pine, birch, beech, oak, maple, hickory, and elm trees grew in the dense forests. The trees provided materials for tools, houses, and canoes, as well as food such as nuts, fruits, and maple sap. Rice, berries, and onions grew wild. The forests were also the habitat of bear, moose, deer, small game animals, and birds. Hunters captured sea mammals along the seacoast while the lakes, rivers, and marshes provided fish. Groups such as the Abenaki trained dogs to help with the hunt.

Early Cultures of the Southwest

Three ancient cultures emerged in the Southwest region at least two thousand years ago. The Mogollon lived along the rivers of western New Mexico and eastern Arizona. At first they lived in pit houses and later built large apartment-like structures of river stone and adobe. The Anasazi, ancestors of the Hopi, built cliff houses in the Four Corners area of Arizona, New Mexico, Utah, and Colorado. The Cliff Palace at Mesa Verde, Colorado, includes two hundred rooms and is the largest cliff dwelling in the United States. The Hohokam settled in central Arizona and were the likely ancestors of the Pima. Like the Mogollon and Anasazi, Hohokam first built pit houses but later constructed complex aboveground structures. One of the best examples is the Great House at Casa Grande. The Hohokam traded with civilizations of central Mexico and adopted elements of their culture. For example, the Hohokam built public ball courts. The largest is at the ancient village of Snaketown in Arizona, and it might have accommodated at least five hundred spectators on the raised sidelines.

Each of the three cultures was highly advanced in agriculture. They created terraced fields and hundreds of miles of irrigation canals to water their crops. Water was a precious resource in southwestern societies, and even young children had to follow strict rules about its use. The Mogollon culture began to decline at the beginning of the twelfth century, and some may have joined the Anasazi or Hohokam. Within a century

Once home to the Anasazi people, the Cliff Palace at Mesa Verde, Colorado, is the largest cliff dwelling in the United States.

the Hohokam and Anasazi experienced a decline that was probably due to soil depletion from centuries of use, overpopulation, a lengthy drought leading to crop failure, widespread hunger, and conflicts. Researchers suggest that the Hohokam abandoned their villages and returned to hunting and gathering, while the Anasazi moved south and east.

The weather was hot and humid in summer, and the winters were cold, with deep snows, but it was suitable for farming. Tribes used sophisticated techniques such as planting mixed crops, including beans, squash, corn, and gourds, or allowing fields to rest for a season or two. Shelters ranged from skin, bark, or cattail-mat-covered wigwams of the Great Lakes area to the longhouses of the Iroquois that housed several families from one clan. In some areas the villages were small, and in others they were spread out over several acres. Like everything else in the Northeast woodlands, the social organization was diverse. The people of some nations lived in villages led by tribal councils headed by a chief. The most complex organization was the League of the Iroquois, which was a confederation of first five and then six Native American nations. The league was based on a constitution and did such things as determine trade policy, set up alliances, and determine how to select leaders.

Iroquois longhouses were large enough to house several families from one clan.

The mythology of the region was as diverse as the other elements of the cultures. Trickster stories, animal myths, nature myths, clan myths, and culture heroes were included.

Their creation stories were exquisite examples of earth-diver myths, which are a kind of creation story.

In contrast to the Northeast woodlands, the environment of the Southeast region was more uniform, with mild winters and plenty of rainfall. Groups such as the Cherokee, Chickasaw, and Creek occupied the northern area. The Natchez and Seminole peoples lived in the south. Pine, oak, and many types of deciduous trees dominated inland forests, while cypress trees thrived in the huge swamps and bayous. There were many food resources available. Game animals included deer, rabbits, squirrels, beaver, and turkeys. Fish, and shellfish were plentiful. Wild food plants such as walnuts, acorns, chestnuts, grapes, persimmons, and many berries were widespread. People made sweet syrup from the sap of certain trees, and bees provided honey. Many groups also farmed corn, beans, and squash. Lifestyles of the southern tribes were varied. The Chickasaw were hunter-gatherers who lived in small camps. The Creek lived in structured villages with separate homes for summer and winter. Their houses had thatched roofs and long porches. Cherokee villages could be home to as many as five hundred people. Most large villages were governed by a council of warriors and elders presided over by a chief. The people of the Southeast shared a complex set of beliefs about the world. Their collective mythologies included origin and animal stories, and the wolf is a prominent character in many myths.

Overall the North American continent provides every imaginable type of climate, landscape, and environment. The diversity of Native American mythology expresses this fact. Nonetheless, although the details and characters may vary from region to region and from culture to culture, the universal themes in the mythology of the First Peoples may be loosely divided into three main groups: creation and origin myths, hero myths, and trickster stories.

CHAPTER 2

The Universal Myths

Since myths often explained how things worked and how humans should behave, they were extremely valuable and contributed to the success of early American tribes. The mythology was closely linked to Native American spirituality, which included a basic belief that all life and all earthly experience was influenced by a divine force. According to Native Net's Native American Mythology website, "This force that they refer to as *The Great Mystery* is prevalent in one way or another in a lot of the stories passed down in history as Native American mythology."[6] The belief in a divine force was often seen in the creation myths.

Creation Stories

In a variety of forms certain elements appear regularly in these myths, such as the presence of a deity or animals that speak, transform, or have unique abilities. The universal aspect is that all creation stories explain how the world began and how people, plants, and animals entered the world. In some cultures only elders or medicine people are permitted to tell creation stories because the power released by the telling of such myths had the ability to "heal, cure, prolong life, and ward off evil,"[7] according to the Indian Country

A chief tells eager listeners a creation myth, which Native Americans used to explain how the world began and how people, plants, and animals entered the world.

website on Native American oral traditions. The person who spoke or performed the creation myth was thought to create a sacred environment. Author Kurt Hübner explains, "By *living* the myths one emerges from profane, chronological time and enters a time that is of a different quality, a *sacred* Time."[8] The words invoked the time of the events that the myth described, and as a result the speaker was in the company of the creator.

There are two main types of creation myths: the emergence story and the earth-diver story. In emergence myths the universe was typically made up of several levels. Humans, or sometimes animals that had human traits, usually lived in the lowest underground level. As conditions changed, the inhabitants climbed up level after level until they emerged through an opening onto the surface of Earth. There are several variations of the Navajo creation myth. In one the First World was a dark place far below the surface. It was home to important beings, including First Man, First Woman, Salt Woman, Fire God, Coyote, and the very powerful Begochiddy, son of the Sun. Begochiddy controlled many things. He created plants such as reeds and sunflowers and four kinds of ants, red, black, gray, and yellow, as well as many other insects. He also created four mountains, black in the north, white in the east, blue in the south, and yellow in the west. He completed his design with a tall red mountain at the center. According to the myth, Fire God was jealous and set the First World aflame. Begochiddy placed a tall reed at the top of the red mountain and encouraged all of the inhabitants to climb up. They left the dark world behind and entered the Second World, which was blue. Begochiddy continued to create new beings, including Cat People, but the residents grew tired of that world, and they climbed higher to the yellow Third World, a beautiful place with rivers and glowing mountains that filled it with light. Finally Begochiddy created humans who all spoke the same language, but it was not long before they began to argue. When Coyote stole the child of a water monster, the monster sent storms and a great flood raced through the Third World. The people gathered around the tall reed and tried to climb up again, but it did not reach the surface. With the help of Spider, Ant, and Locust they finally broke through and emerged onto the Fourth World. They continued upward and emerged in the Fifth World, on the surface of Earth, but it was covered with water. Badger tried to dig up some land but he sank in the mud, and to this day badgers have black paws. Begochiddy encouraged the winds to dry the land, and the people were able to spread out. He made the sun and the moon while First Man, First Woman, and Coyote gathered up shiny stones and placed them in the sky to serve as stars. Begochiddy gave humans stories that explained how to give thanks and how to care for the plants. He gave them different languages and sent them to live all around the world. Begochiddy also gave a warning that as long as animals and humans lived the right way, in harmony and balance, all would be well, but if they did not, their world, like the others, would face destruction. Some medicine men claim that there are two worlds above the Fifth World: the World of the Spirits of Living Things and the Place of Melting into One.

Earth-Diver Myths

An earth-diver myth also depicts a multilayered world that often included an underworld, a natural world, and a sky world. In this myth Earth was covered by water and populated by animals. When a being fell from the sky above, one or more of the animals attempted to build an island so that the being would not drown. One of the animal earth-divers would be successful in bringing up enough mud to start the island-building process. As the island expanded, plants started to grow on it. In one version a turtle offered to support the island on its back, and some cultures referred to North America as Turtle Island. In many earth-diver stories a central element such as a sacred mountain, a pillar, or a totem pole connected the layers. This connection is known as an axis mundi, and it was a point at which a powerful medicine person or shaman was able to move from one level to another to gain knowledge. A tree could also represent the axis mundi with its branches reaching to the sky, its trunk touching the earth, and its roots reaching the underworld. An earth-diver myth that incorporated a tree is represented in the Iroquois creation myth of Sky Woman.

In this story humans were of a divine origin and first lived on the uppermost, or heavenly, level. The earth below was covered with water. There were no dry lands, islands, or mountains. There were plenty of fish and sea creatures, but the only living beings on the surface were waterbirds and sea-going animals. High above the water was Skyland where the Sky People lived. They were led by a powerful chief. His pretty young wife was soon to give birth to a child. One night she had a dream about the Great Tree that grew at the center of Sky Land. It was a huge, majestic tree, but the young woman dreamed that it must be pulled up. When she told her husband about this he decided that the dream was an omen of power. He gathered many people together, and they carefully uprooted the tree and tipped it to one side, exposing a gigantic hole. The people stared down through the tangle of roots and saw

Native American Monsters

The popularity of the Stephenie Meyers series *Twilight* has drawn attention to the mythology of the Quileute (KWIL yoot) people of western Washington. According to Meyers, the Apotamkin, described as a vampire in the story, is fictional. In fact, the Apotamkin is a mythological monster of the Maliseet and Passamaquoddy tribes of the Northeast. The myth was used to convince children not to venture too close to dangerous bodies of water alone. A huge fanged sea serpent with long red hair, the Apotamkin was said to lie in wait in the Passamaquoddy Bay. It would pounce on unsuspecting victims and drag them into the water.

Another element in the *Twilight* series is actually a traditional part of Quileute mythology. According to the story, the people of the tribe were descended from wolves that were transformed into men by a supernatural being. The name Quileute is drawn from *kwoli*, the native term for wolf. In the American Southwest, the Navajo and other tribes have stories of shape-shifters called skinwalkers. The evil beings were usually witches capable of transforming into wolves or other animals. A witch began by wearing the hide of the creature and absorbing its traits, such as speed and strength, as well as supernatural abilities including immunity to most weapons, mind-reading ability, and the ability to control people who make eye contact. The skin walker was vulnerable in its human form and could easily be killed, but in its animal form the only way to destroy it was with a sacred weapon created by a medicine man.

the watery world below. The chief's curious young wife leaned too far, and she slid down, falling through the gaping hole. She tried to save herself by grabbing for a root, but she could not hold on and slipped away with only a handful of seeds.

Two swans flying below saw the terrified woman plummeting toward the sea. They raced to catch her, but all they could manage to do was slow her fall. Far below, Duck, Loon, Beaver, and Muskrat dove beneath the waters to gather

The World Tree

An example of an axis mundi is Yggdrasil, the World Tree, which joins the nine worlds of Norse mythology such as Asgard and Midgard. Also called the tree of fate, it is usually described as a huge ash tree. Its three huge roots descend into the underworld and reach three wells, including the well of wisdom and the well of fate.

mud to make an island for her so that she would not drown. They tried over and over again but could not dive deep enough. Finally Muskrat managed to bring up a pawful of dark mud. Great Turtle paddled close and told Muskrat to smear the mud on his shell. The thin smear grew wider and thicker to become an island on Great Turtle's back. Sky Woman landed gently. She dug a small hole and planted the seeds in the soil. They immediately sprouted and spread throughout the new land. The first was strawberry and the second was tobacco. Not long after, Sky Woman gave birth to a daughter who later became the mother of twin sons. One was evil. The other was good and became the father of humankind.

The story of Sky Woman is one in which people and animals began life on the surface of Earth in harmony through an act of goodness. Not all creation myths ended so well. Olelbis was the creator god of the Wintun tribe of the California Pacific Coast. He was known as The Great One Who Sits Above The Sky in a place called Olelpanti. Olelbis began by creating a race of humans. He wanted them to live happily and in peace without sickness, birth, or death, but they argued and fought. Two tribes began a terrible war. They started so many fires that all corners of the earth burned at once. Olelbis was sad when he looked down at the flames. Even the rocks and ground were burning. Olelbis sent wind and rain to put out the fire, and he restored the earth and turned the humans into other things like trees, fish, and birds. The creator god still wanted humans to live forever and join him in Olelpanti, so he created a new race. To make it easier for the new people to reach him he sent two brother vultures to build a stone road to Olelpanti. At the end of the road there were to be two springs. When a human grew old he could travel up the road, bathe in one spring, and drink from the other to become young again.

When Sedit the Coyote Man saw this he was annoyed at the way that humans were being favored. He convinced the vultures that it was not a good idea for humans to live forever. He talked them into stopping their work and destroying the road. Because of this act, death entered the world. Much to his dismay, Sedit learned the he would also have to die someday. To escape his fate he decided to fly to Olelpanti. He built a pair of wings from sunflower leaves and tied them to his shoulders. Climbing to a high peak he took to the air, but the leaves withered as he neared the sun. He crashed to Earth and became the first to die. Olelbis saw all of this and said, "Sedit is the first of all living things to die. He has been killed by his own words. From this time on, all men will die. They will know the gladness of birth. They will know the sorrow of death. And through these two things together men will come to know love."[9]

Origin Myths

Origin myths explained how things came to be the way they were. Native Americans traditionally lived in harmony with nature. Many believed that the animals that shared the earth with them could be messengers from the spirit world. A common idea in Native American mythology is that animals were once able to speak to humans, change their physical form at will, and that each species embodied a particular spirit power. One result of this point of view is the major role animals often played in myths. They regularly assisted people by sharing important knowledge and survival skills. Origin myths often explained how animals came to look and behave the way they did, and how the relationship between human and animal evolved. For example, the Shasta people told that Earth was once a woman. The Great Creator turned her flesh into soil, her bones to rock, and her breath to wind. The deity then rolled balls of soil in his hands and made them living beings, some human, some animals, and some that were blends of animal and human. The result was humans that could fly or dive deep into the oceans and animals that had human speech and other traits. This blending helped humans learn to respect all nature.

Many cultures have cautionary tales about what happens when humans lose their respect for other living things. According to this Cherokee origin myth, animals angry about their treatment at human hands were responsible for the origin of disease. In the early days of Earth the humans, animals, and even plants could speak to each other, and they lived in peace. As the human population grew they took over more and more land and crowded the animals out. When humans developed weapons they began hunting and eating the animals. Even the tiniest frogs and worms suffered because humans would crush them underfoot without a thought. At last the animals gathered together to talk about what they could do to protect themselves.

The bears thought that people should stop hunting animals. They suggested threatening humans by using man's own weapons against him. They created a bow and some arrows but could not shoot the arrows because their long claws tangled in the bowstring. The bears tried cutting their claws and that made it easier to use the bow, but without claws they could not climb trees. They decided it was better to rely on the weapons that nature had given them, teeth and claws.

Deer spoke next. He proposed that if people were going to hunt animals, they should at least be respectful. Deer suggested that they should sicken any hunter who killed one of them and ate the meat without first asking for pardon. A deer spirit could strike a disrespectful hunter with a crippling disease. The fish and reptiles agreed that it was a good idea. They planned to give humans horrifying dreams about slithering snakes and decaying fish so that humans would be unable to eat and would sicken and die. The birds, insects, and other small animals thought up so many diseases and ailments they could inflict on humans that it seemed like none would survive.

Fortunately for people, the plants were still their friends. When Tree, Shrub, Herb, Grass, and Moss learned of the plans the animals had, they decided to help humans. Every plant developed a healing remedy, but people had to learn how to use them. When a healer did not know what medicine to use for an illness, if he or she listened respectfully, the spirit of the plant would whisper the answer. And that is how medicine came to be.

The knowledge of plant medicine was critical to Native Americans. Mythology not only included origin myths about how such things came into being, but some myths explained how they should be used. The stories of cultural heroes often served this purpose. The characters in these myths shared important knowledge that helped humans to survive in their environment. Heroes taught the people how

The Story of Icarus

Sedit's disastrous attempt to fly to Olelpanti was similar to the Greek myth of Icarus, son of Daedalus. The story began when King Minos of Crete asked Daedalus to build an underground labrynth, or maze, a structure with winding passages designed to confuse anyone trying to find their way in or out. It was intended to hold a half-man half-bull beast known as the Minotaur. Over many years Minos had demanded that the city of Athens send young men to Crete as a tribute. They were then fed to the creature. When a young man named Theseus came to battle the Minotaur, Minos's daughter, Ariadne, fell in love with him. She asked Daedalus to help her save him. He gave her a ball of string, which she smuggled to Theseus. By following the string the young man found his way out of the labrynth after killing the monster. Theseus and Ariadne escaped Crete together. This enraged Minos who locked Daedalus and Icarus in a tower in the Palace of Knossos. Using wax and feathers, Daedalus created two pairs of wings that enabled them to fly to

According to the Greek myth, Daedalus and Icarus used wings to fly to freedom, but Icarus crashed after flying too close to the sun.

freedom. He warned his son not to fly too close to the sun, but Icarus was thrilled to be able to soar through the sky. He dipped and whirled and flew as high as he could. When he became careless and flew too close to the sun, the wax melted and the feathers dropped off similarly to the way that the sun withered the leaves of Sedit's wings. Icarus crashed into the water below and drowned in the area that now bears his name, the Icarian Sea.

A variety of traditional Native American medicinal plants are collected for display. Mythology explains how native people acquired and learned to use these plants, which were critical to their existence.

to perform rituals and ceremonies, and they brought gifts of incredible value such as fire and rain. They represented the best of a culture and possessed the qualities that the society valued. They made the world a better, safer place for their people. The cultural heroes of Native American mythology set an example of what people should try to be and do. Such heroes were sometimes supernatural in origin, and they may have had magical abilities. The cultural heroes could also be a blend of hero, creator, or trickster.

Glooskap

One of the most important cultural heroes of the Northeast woodlands was Glooskap, and there are dozens of myths about him. Though his name and the details of his life vary widely among tribes, the myths about Glooskap are well known among Algonquian-speaking people such as the

Abenaki, Micmac, and Penobscot. He was said to be the First Man, and he created himself from dust that Tabaldak the Creator had brushed from his hands after making the world. Glooskap continued the work of Tabaldak by creating the animals. Even as a very young child he showed his magical abilities. Glooskap lived with Grandmother Woodchuck, who gave him a special fur bag made from her own belly fur. Since then woodchucks have no fur on their bellies. The bag held an endless number of animals and could never be filled. One day the young boy decided that he was tired of people hunting and wanted to protect the creatures of the forest. He went to the animals and told them that they could hide in his fur bag where they would be safe. When he told Grandmother Woodchuck what he had done, she shook her head and told him that hiding the creatures was wrong. She explained that without animals of the forest the people

The Spirit Wife

Native Americans had different views of life after death. Some believed that the dead became spirits or ghosts. Others believed that the dead were reborn in human or animal form. Zuni mythology described a land where human spirits went after death. In one myth a man was so grief stricken by the death of his young wife that he could not bear to let her go. He decided to follow her spirit as she crossed into the land of the dead and bring her back. Because spirits were invisible he attached a red feather to her hair as she was prepared for burial. Following the feather, he trailed after his wife's spirit. When she crossed a frigid lake the feather disappeared. The man thought he had lost her, but an owl gave him a special potion. The owl explained that it would make him sleep. When he awoke he would be able to see his wife, and she would follow him to the land of the living. The owl also warned him not to touch her until they were back in their village. All went as planned, but the man was so happy as they neared their village that he reached out and touched his wife's arm, and she slipped back to the land of the dead. This type of story is called an Orphic myth because it is similar to a Greek myth about a young man named Orpheus who traveled to the underworld to retrieve his dead wife. The god Hades gave him permission to take her but warned that he must not look at her until they were in the living world. Orpheus looked back to be certain his wife was following, and so, like the Zuni man, he lost his wife forever.

A mother and child are visited by Glooskap, a common character in the mythology of tribes from the Northeast woodlands who is described as the First Man.

would starve. Glooskap learned that doing the right thing was not always simple.

As he became a man his powers and skills grew. He is credited with teaching humans correct hunting and fishing skills as well as important crafts such as tanning hides, weaving, and beadwork. When the time came for Glooskap to leave his people, he held a great feast on the shores of Lake Minas. The guests included all of the animals who at the time spoke the same language. When the feast was over, the hero climbed into his canoe and sang as he paddled away. As the sound of his voice faded the animals could no longer understand each other. Filled with fear they raced away. According to the story, they will never sit in friendship again until Glooskap returns, which he will do when his people need him. Cultural heroes often left promises or warnings for their people. This was true of an important cultural hero of the Cheyenne nation named Arrow Boy.

Arrow Boy

Cheyenne mythology includes the story of an orphaned boy named Motzeyouf, who later became known as Arrow Boy. Even as a child he had great magical abilities that rivaled those of the most powerful medicine men. He could take the form of animals and make buffalo appear and disappear. When the boy killed a chief during an argument, the people became afraid of him and threatened him. Motzeyouf vanished, taking the buffalo with him. He left the tribe and traveled to a holy mountain in the Black Hills. The mountain had a door in its side. Inside, a group of elders invited him to join them, and they taught him many things, including sacred songs and ceremonies. He spent four years learning all that he could. Before he left the mountain the elders gave him a medicine bundle and four sacred arrows. When Motzeyouf returned as Arrow Boy, he found his people starving because he had made the buffalo disappear. He performed a ritual with the four sacred arrows and taught the people four songs to sing. When they finished singing the people heard what sounded like thunder. By morning the herds had returned by the thousands. Arrow Boy instructed the people to take from the herd only what they needed and promised they would never be hungry again.

In one variation of the myth, as an old man Arrow Boy told his people to "beware the light-skinned strangers. They will bring sicknesses of all kind to you."[10] He said the strangers would bring what seemed like marvelous gifts, but they would make the people forget their past and their ancestors. He warned that the greedy strangers would kill for yellow stones and "turn the whole world into stone."[11] Once more Arrow Boy disappeared, never to be seen again. In another version of this tale the hero is named Sweet Medicine. As his death drew near the people took him to the base of the mountain where he had learned from the elders. Modern Cheyenne identify the mountain as the Devil's Tower in Wyoming and consider it a sacred place.

The Tricksters

Heroes may occasionally be tricksters. Native American myths are filled with tricksters, crafty, clever, and sometimes comical figures that did things to help or to hinder others. The trickster represented uncertainty, something that most Native Americans knew well and took in stride. Tricksters brought benefits and caused mischief. They could be human, but they were often animals that played tricks on others and sometimes became victims of their own bad behavior. The characters in this type of myth included Rabbit, Fox, and Skunk, all small animals that were cunning rather than strong. The most common tricksters were Raven and Coyote. Many Arctic, subarctic, and Northwest coastal tribes viewed Raven as a culture hero. He could be a kindly figure who often helped people. Even so, Raven was a trickster character, and his behavior sometimes caused trouble. Since tricksters often behaved poorly

A carving portrays the head of a raven, a common character in the mythology of tribes from the Arctic, subarctic, and Northwest coastal regions who was often portrayed as a trickster.

and broke taboos, trickster myths demonstrate that there was a steep price to pay when rules were broken. Tricksters appeared in nearly all Native American mythologies, but they were very common among hunter-gatherer peoples.

To the Karok of the California region, Coyote was a trickster but earned the respect of the people by bringing them fire. Because of his warm fur he had no need for it himself, but one day he passed a village where humans were mourning the loss of children and elderly people who had died because of the bitter cold of winter. Coyote felt sorry for them and tried to come up with a way to help. He thought of a time that he had seen three Fire Beings with glittering eyes and long claws on a distant mountaintop. He knew the Fire Beings were selfish and would not be willing to share fire with the humans. Although he could easily walk on two legs, Coyote trotted up the mountain on all fours to watch for a while and think about what to do.

As he came near their fire, the Fire Beings jumped up and stared into the forest. When they saw Coyote standing in the shadows they smiled, knowing a furred animal had no use for fire. Coyote watched as night fell. The Fire Beings began to yawn, and two crawled into their tepee to sleep. As the hours passed, the Fire Beings took turns guarding the flames. At dawn Coyote noticed that the guard was sleepy and its eyelids looked heavy. The guard headed for the tepee, calling for its replacement to come out. Coyote saw his chance, raced forward, and scooped up some flickering flames in his mouth. The fire was warm but did not burn him. As the Fire Beings screamed in anger, Coyote took off down the mountain. The Fire Beings charged after him, and at the bottom of the mountain one of them grabbed at his tail. When Coyote yelped, the fire leaped from his mouth and jumped into a piece of wood. The Fire Beings tried to get the flame out of the wood but could not. With a snarl they turned and headed back up the mountain. Coyote knew how to get fire out of the wood. He showed the people of the village how to

The Tricksters

Tricksters such as Coyote appear in myths and legends around the world. The Scandinavian god Loki was a shape-shifter who caused trouble for the other gods. Anansi the Spider of West Africa was clever and mischievous, and in Japanese tales, the fox is featured as a shape-shifting trickster hero.

rub two sticks together until smoke appeared and fire finally jumped out. Coyote had played a trick on the Fire Beings, and humans had fire to warm themselves in winter.

In each Native American mythology, beings such as Sky Woman, Coyote, and Glooskap played an important spiritual role, but they were not gods or demigods as they might be considered in other mythologies of the world. Perhaps the most difficult concept about the Native American belief system for non-Indians to understand is their concept of divinity.

CHAPTER 3

Deities and Spirits

The spiritualities of every group of Native Americans cannot be lumped into a single belief system, but there is a thread that ran through most cultures. It was the acceptance of a divine spirit that permeated everything, both spiritual and physical. To the Cree that spirit was called Manitou, which authors David Leeming and Jake Page describe as "the primeval force or all-encompassing power of the universe that created the universe. In turn, each and every animal, plant and rock, its power and character, contain this living spirit."[12] Evidence of this spirit was seen in everything: the change of seasons; birth and death; and the movement of the sun, moon, and stars. The Lakota Sioux had a similar concept, which they called *wakan* (holy or sacred). This concept is difficult, so Native American myths generally included a personification of the divine spirit that they called the Great Spirit or Great Mystery. Scholars describe such a personification as a creator deity, one of the most important beings in a mythology. This is the supreme being who brought the universe or Earth into existence. The creator deity may sometimes be personified as the Sun or the Sky. In Zuni mythology the creator deity is Awonawilona, The One Who Contains Everything. This being, who was described as both male and female, was said to exist when there was nothing but darkness and emptiness. Awonawilona created everything from himself and took the form of the Sun, the Maker of Light.

Tirawa was the creator god of the Pawnee people of the Great Plains. He gave them fire, hunting, agriculture, and speech, and he taught them many important rituals. According to the Pawnee, Tirawa created the world and directed four stars to support the sky. After he gave the Sun and Moon their power, their marriage resulted in the First Man. Tirawa also created the Morning Star and Evening Star, which married and gave birth to the First Woman. When Tirawa gave some of the brighter stars in the sky control of the clouds, winds, and rain, his actions angered some of the dim stars. They found a bag of ferocious storms that a bright star had set aside, opened it, and dumped the storms on Earth, bringing tragedy and death.

The Pawnee honored Tirawa by observing the sky. A Pawnee village sometimes included huge lodges that could each house thirty or more people. The construction included four painted poles, which represented the four directions and the four most important star deities. A smoke hole in the center allowed the people inside to view the sky. The Pawnee performed certain ceremonies and planted their crops based on the positions of the stars.

To the Lakota people, Wakan Tanka is the creator. Before time began, there was only Wakan Tanka in a great, dark emptiness. When the creator decided to will the universe into being, he began by forming Ínyan, or Rock, the first of the important beings, then from Ínyan he created Maka, the Earth goddess sometimes called Grandmother Earth. He next created Sky, which brought forth the Sun. These deities were separate and powerful, but they were also part of Wakan Tanka. In turn they created the Moon, Wind, Falling Star, and Thunderbird. All of these spirits and elements of nature are aspects of Wakan Tanka.

In some myths the supreme being begins the process of creation and then disappears or distances himself, leaving other beings to complete the work of creation. The secondary beings are often personifications of natural forces such as the wind.

The Hero's Journey

Joseph Campbell (1904–1987) was an American mythologist who wrote several books on the power of myth, including *The Hero with A Thousand Faces* (1949) and *The Masks of God* (1968). Campbell also made a popular 1988 documentary with journalist Bill Moyers, *The Power of Myth*. As a child, Campbell was fascinated by Native American mythology. This led him to a lifelong study of myth. After comparing the stories of many cultures, Campbell outlined a blueprint for classic heroic behavior called the hero's journey, found in myths around the world. In *The Hero with a Thousand Faces*, Campbell discusses this pattern, or monomyth. "A hero ventures forth from the world of common day into a region of supernatural wonder: fabulous forces are there encountered and a decisive victory is won: the hero comes back from this mysterious adventure with the power to bestow boons on his fellow man."

Many modern films such as Disney's *The Lion King* (1994) and *Aladdin* (1992) are based on this monomyth. Director George Lucas incorporated the hero's journey and other classic motifs in his blockbuster film series Star Wars (1977) and Indiana Jones (1981). The pattern can also be seen in beloved children's books from *Huckleberry Finn* and *The Wizard of Oz* to *The Hobbit* and the Harry Potter series.

Joseph Campbell. *The Hero with a Thousand Faces*. Princeton, NJ: Princeton University Press, 1949, p. 23.

Mother Corn and Spider Woman

In some mythologies a creator may work in partnership with a female deity sometimes represented as Mother Earth, who gives birth to and provides for all living things. This is known as a world parent myth. A typical form of world parent myth involves the death and dismemberment of a powerful, primeval being. Parts of the being's body

The National Air and Space Museum sponsored an exhibit from 1997 to 1999 called *Star Wars: The Magic of Myth*. More than two hundred props and costumes were on display, including the light sabers of Luke Skywalker and Darth Vader. The exhibit focused on how Star Wars films were influenced by Joseph Cambell's books.

become Earth itself, as well as earthly geological features, animals, or important crops.

The Penobscot of the Northeast woodlands relate the story of their world parent, Mother Corn. It begins with Kloskurbeh, a figure identified with Glooskap of the Algonquian myths. Kloskurbeh was also known as the All Maker. He walked on Earth and was very happy with all of the beauty that he saw, but he was lonely. One day he saw a young man walking toward him. The man called him Uncle and explained that he had been born from wave foam, wind, and the warmth of the sun. Kloskurbeh was pleased. He made the young man his helper, and they continued to create many different things. Again Kloskurbeh saw a figure in the distance and watched as a young woman approached. She explained that she had been born of the earth's plants and dew. The young man and woman were married and soon had human children, making the girl First Mother. Kloskurbeh was pleased, and he taught the humans all that they needed to know and how to live well. Satisfied, Kloskurbeh decided it was time for him to leave, promising to return when he was needed.

At first the people lived well. They hunted and showed respect for the earth. Over time their population grew and they needed more meat, so they took more animals. It became difficult to find game, and people began to starve. First Mother was sad for her children, but there was something she could do. She instructed her husband to kill her, drag her body over a wide empty field, bury her bones there, and leave. She explained that seven moons later her flesh would bloom from love, and it would nourish her children forever. With tears in his eyes, her husband did as she asked. When he and his children returned at the appointed time, the field was covered with tall green plants topped with ears of plump, sweet corn. They ate what they needed and saved kernels to plant so that Mother Corn would always provide food for her children.

Mother Corn is a form of the dying god concept. In such stories a deity dies and returns in a way that can benefit the people. The Cherokee myth of Selu, or Corn Mother, is another version of this tale. In some areas Cherokee farmers would bury a few fish in their fields as a gift to thank First Mother for her sacrifice.

In one form or another, Spider Woman appears in the myths of several tribes, including the Pawnee, Cherokee, Choctaw, Keres, and Navajo. She is a primordial deity of the Hopi people of the Southwest region. According to their myth, at the beginning of time there were no people or animals or plants. There was only the sun god Tawa and the earth goddess Spider Woman. Tawa controlled the sky, and Spider Woman controlled the underworld. Using only their thoughts, the two beings created Earth. Spider Woman shaped animals from clay. Together with Tawa she covered them with a blanket and whispered magic words that brought them to life. Next she shaped humans from clay and sang over them to bring them to life.

In another version of the Hopi myth, Tawa created insect beings to occupy the First World. He was not happy with his creation, so he sent Spider Woman to lead them. She guided them upward through the Second World to the Third World, where they became human. Spider Woman taught the people many skills, including weaving and pottery making. When evil entered the Third World, Spider Woman told the people to plant a tall reed and sing to it to make it grow. When it was tall enough, the people climbed it and emerged into the Fourth World.

In some myths Spider Woman had a dangerous side, but she was usually kind and generous. She helped humans to learn important skills, including how to sow seeds and how to use fire and keep it safe. Spider Woman also taught the Navajo how to spin and weave cotton and wool. Navajo are known worldwide for this skill. "Before weavers sit down at the loom, they often rub their hands in spider webs to absorb the wisdom and skill of Spider Woman."[13]

Cultural Deities: White Buffalo Woman and Sedna

A cultural deity is a key figure who brings a tribe its major customs and spiritual insights. These deities teach people how to survive spiritually and physically in the world. In many cases the important rituals and ceremonies of a group are given by a cultural deity.

The Sacred Pipe Ceremony was the most basic of all the ceremonies of the Lakota people, and it was the basis for all other ceremonies. The story of White Buffalo Woman is a central myth of the Lakota that tells how they first received their sacred pipe. One summer the seven council fires of the Lakota nation had camped together. Chief Standing Hollow Horn was among them. There was little game in the area, and hunters were sent out every day to search for food. In the early morning two young men decided they would go out to hunt. They set off across the plain and walked and walked. The day became warm, and the intense sunlight caused the distant horizon to look hazy. The young men climbed a small hill to get a better look. Shielding their eyes, they searched in every direction. All at once they saw a figure in the distance. At first they thought it might be an animal but soon saw that it was a woman who appeared to float rather than walk. One of the men realized that the she must be a holy being. As the woman drew closer, they saw that she was dressed in white buckskin that glowed in the sun. It was embroidered with sacred designs made of porcupine quills in all the colors of the rainbow. Her long dark hair hung loosely except for a strand that was tied with buffalo fur. She carried a bundle on her back and held a fan of sage leaves.

One of the two men was amazed by the woman's beauty. He smiled at his friend and said that he would like to claim her as his own. The wise young man warned him that the woman was holy and should be shown great respect. The foolish man

---

Spider Rock in Canyon de Chelly, Arizona, is considered by the Navajo people to be the home of Spider Woman, a prominent character in their mythology.

ignored the advice. When the woman was near enough, he reached out to touch her. From a clear sky a bolt of lightning crackled down, and a dark cloud swirled around him. When the cloud lifted the woman was standing nearby, but all that was left of the disrespectful young man was a blackened pile of bones with snakes slithering among them. The respectful young man was frightened, but she soothed his fears and told him that she wished to visit the Lakota camp to bring them something holy and a message from Tatanka Oyate, the buffalo nation. She told him to run ahead and tell Chief Standing Hollow Horn what had happened and to prepare a medicine lodge large enough for all his people to gather inside.

The man raced back across the prairie and quickly told the chief everything that had happened. The chief followed the instructions that had been given. After four days a scout brought the news that the holy woman was approaching. Then she was suddenly walking among them. After she examined the interior of the medicine lodge, she pointed to a place where the people built a sacred altar made of red earth for the holy gift that she had brought. When the altar was complete she unrolled the bundle and took out a beautiful pipe. The bowl was red stone like the earth. The face of a buffalo calf, representing all four-legged animals, was carved into the stone. Engraved in the bowl were seven circles to stand for the seven ceremonies and the seven campfires of the Lakota nation. The stem was wood to represent all that grows on the earth. Twelve spotted eagle feathers hung from the stem to stand for all the winged creatures. White Buffalo Woman told the people that when they smoked the pipe they must remember that all living things are one family with humans. She taught them the right way to pray, how to sing the pipe-filling song, and how to lift the pipe to honor Great Spirit, Father Sky, and Mother Earth. White Buffalo Woman explained that four ages were coming, and she promised to return at the end of the fourth. She walked away

The White Buffalo

In 1994 a white buffalo was born on a farm in Wisconsin. Named Miracle, she died in 2004. In 2006 a male white buffalo was born on the same farm and named Miracle's Second Chance. Jim Matheson of the National Bison Association points out that the odds of a white buffalo birth are at least one in a million.

and sat down on the prairie. When she rose, she was a red and brown buffalo calf. The creature took a few steps then rolled on the ground. When it stood, it was a black buffalo calf. She repeated her roll once more and stood as a white buffalo calf, then bowed to the four directions and disappeared. According to author Mary C. Churchill, "White Buffalo Calf Woman and the buffalo in general remain the center of Lakota cultural survival. In fact, the birth of several rare white buffalos in the 1990s signaled to some Lakotas [her] return."[14]

Some Lakota consider the birth of a rare white buffalo in modern times to be a sign of the return of the mythological White Buffalo Woman.

Sedna

Not all cultural deities are benevolent. Sedna is an angry goddess and one of the most significant figures in Inuit mythology. There are many versions of the myth, but they all have similar elements. Sedna was a beautiful young girl who lived with her father. She knew she was lovely and that many young men wanted to marry her, but she turned up her nose at all of them. She found fault with every offer until her father became angry. He told her that he would not always be there to take care of her, so she would have to marry the next man who asked. It was not long before a hunter approached. He wore fine clothes and furs, but his face was hidden in his hood. Sedna's father introduced his daughter to the man and said that she would be a fine wife. The girl was furious, but when the hunter agreed, she was forced to sit behind him in his kayak. He had paddled in silence for a long time when a barren rocky island came into view. Sedna was stunned. She had expected a nice home. Her husband guided the kayak onto the barren windswept shore, stood, and pulled down his hood. Horrified, Sedna saw that he was not a hunter but a raven in disguise.

She tried to run, but there was nowhere to go. The raven dragged her to his nest high on a cliff and left her with nothing to eat but raw fish. Every day he flew off to fish, leaving her alone sobbing in misery. She cried out her father's name so loudly that he finally heard her over the howling wind. Feeling guilty, her father took to sea in his kayak, following the sound of Sedna's voice. When he arrived, Sedna was standing on the rocky shore. She raced to the edge of the frigid water and climbed into the kayak. They had paddled for hours when Sedna heard the angry cries of her husband. She could see him in the distance, flying to reclaim her. When he caught up to them, the raven flew low and beat his wings on the surface of the water, causing a fierce storm. Sedna's father was terrified. To save his own life he grabbed his daughter and threw her into the ocean. Sedna sank, swallowing huge gulps of icy water. She struggled to the surface and swam to the kayak grasping its edge with her fingers and begging her father for help. Instead he battered her with the paddle. Her frozen fingers cracked off and fell into the ocean. As they sank into the sea, Sedna's fingers turned into seals. She reached for the kayak once more, and her father hit her frozen hands and they snapped off. As they sank her hands turned into whales. Unable to hold on any longer, the girl disappeared beneath the surface.

The time Sedna had spent with her magical husband had affected her so she did not drown. Instead she became Mother of Oceans and ruler over all life in the sea, an angry deity known to send violent storms or withhold sea animals

Little People of the Island

Magical little people appear in the myths and legends of dozens of cultures around the world. Nearly every Native American culture has a story of a race of little people such as the Nunnupis of the Comanche and the Nimerigar of the Shoshone people, who were known to use tiny bows and deadly poison-tipped arrows. Hawaiians tell of the Menehune (me neh HOO neh), who were part of Polynesian mythology. It is likely that the Hawaiian Islands were uninhabited when the Polynesians arrived by boat around fifteen hundred years ago. The seafarers probably came by way of the Marquesas Islands, which they may have left because of overpopulation or conflicts. According to their myths, Havaiki was the name of the land where the Polynesian people originated and where their spirits went after death. When they arrived on the big island at Ka Lae on the southern coast, they may have called it Havaiki, which later became Hawaii. When the Polynesians landed they found what they thought were dams, fishponds, and small rock temples. They decided these were the work of Menehune, who hid in the forest and lived in caves. The little people were mischievous, but they were also capable builders. They supposedly built the Alekoko Fishpond located near Lihue, Kauai, in one moonlit night. The lava rock wall that separates the pond from Huleia Stream is 4 feet (1.2m) thick, 5 feet (1.5m) high, and 900 feet (274m) long. The pond was built about one thousand years ago to catch fish and is sometimes called Menehune Fishpond.

According to Polynesian mythology, the Alekoko Fishpond in Kauai, Hawaii, was built by little people known as the Menehune.

from hunters when she was not treated with respect. For this reason, whenever an Inuit hunter caught a seal he would drip water into its mouth to thank Sedna for her generosity. Many aspects of Inuit daily life were designed to calm her. Without her blessing, the Inuit believed that hunts would fail and the people would starve.

Like Corn Mother, Sedna is an example of a dying god myth. Although she did not willingly sacrifice herself for the good of her people, the result is the same. Sedna's broken fingers and hands became the sea mammals that the Inuit relied upon for their survival.

Spirit Figures

Not all mythological beings of North America are powerful deities or even heroes or tricksters. The mythology of the Hopi, Zuni, Keres, and Tewa, of the Southwestern region all included some form of kachina, spirit figures that brought favors or knowledge. The original kachinas were supernatural spirits and beings that represented and had charge over elements of the natural world. According to the Hopi, kachinas were also spirits of departed ancestors who had lived properly. Kachinas were not only spirits of the dead but could be spirits of animals, plants, minerals, stars, and much more. If treated with respect, they would use their individual powers to benefit humans. They could bring rainfall, increase crop yields, ripen corn, heal certain illnesses, and provide protection.

In the Hopi emergence myth, as the people emerged into the Fourth World they came face to face with Massau, a kachina that was the Keeper of the Earth. His permission was required before the Hopi could live on the surface. Other spirits taught the Hopi the skills they needed to survive, such as how to hunt, make tools, and plant crops. The kachinas also taught the Hopi how to heal sickness, how to give thanks, and how to offer prayers. As guardians of the Hopi the kachinas carried the prayers of the people to the spirit world. The Hopi link between the natural world and the spirit world was made by the kachinas.

Myths in the Solar System

Astronomers often name astronomical objects such as planets and moons after mythological beings. Earth is the only planet in the solar system not named after a Greek or Roman god. Native American mythology is represented too. The Tirawa basin, a large impact crater on Saturn's moon Rhea, is named for the creator deity of the Pawnee people. In 2003 a large planetoid was named after Sedna, the Inuit ocean deity. The remote body was discovered near the outer edge of the solar system by astronomers from the California Institute of Technology (CalTech), Yale, and Hawaii's Gemini Observatory. With a surface temperature of about -400°F (-240°C), Sedna is the coldest known object in the solar system. It is also one of the slowest and most distant. It takes about 11,400 years for the planetoid to complete one orbit, and it is never nearer than 8 billion miles (12.9 billion km) away from the sun. The last time Sedna was at its current position in the solar system, Earth was emerging from the last Ice Age. Made up of rocky, icy material, Sedna is one of the smallest planetlike objects, with a diameter of 1,100 miles (1,770km) or about two-thirds the size of Pluto. One category that Sedna stands out in is color. Astronomer Michael E. Brown of CalTech points out that the tiny planetoid is almost as red as Mars.

The planetoid Sedna, named for the Inuit goddess, was discovered in 2003.

Another myth explains the first meeting of the Hopi and the kachinas differently. One summer night during a terrible drought, the people heard singing and dancing in the nearby mountains. When they followed the sounds they discovered that the caves were home to many kachinas. When the people explained that the drought was ruining their crops, the kachinas returned with the Hopi to their villages and danced and sang to bring rain. The kachinas would spend six months of the year in their mountain homes and six months in the villages. The Hopi believed that the dances were crucial to bring rain to the Hopi farms and to maintain the harmony and balance of their land. Eventually the kachinas stopped coming, but they taught the sacred dances to a group of young men who became the first Hopi priests. From then on masked dancers personified the spirits and continued the annual ritual. In magnificent costumes the masked kachina dancers acted as intermediaries between the natural and spirit worlds, to thank the spirits and so ensure such blessings as rain, abundant crops, and success in hunting. Carved and painted kachina dolls were given to Hopi children to help them identify the various spiritual figures and their costumes.

Little People

In the Southeast woodlands, the original home of the Cherokee, there are many myths about the Little People, or Yundi Tsundi, a race of spirits who live in caves in the Appalachian Mountains. They looked much like Cherokee people but were only about two feet tall or even smaller. Their dark hair was so long that it almost brushed the ground. The Little People spoke both Cherokee and a mysterious language of their own. Because they loved music, singing, and dancing, sometimes their drumming could be heard deep in the mountains' most secret places. The Little People could not be seen unless they chose to show themselves, and it was foolish to try to look

Two Hopi dress in kachina costumes to perform a dance to thank and gain the favor of the spirit world.

for them. They could cast a spell over an intruder, causing him to become confused and lose his way. If one of the Little People was accidentally seen or chose to appear to a human, that person was not to speak of the meeting for at least seven years. People also avoided speaking about the Little People after dark. Some Little People were mischievous and liked to play tricks, but they were generally kind and helpful. They taught people joy and respect. According to myth, there was one exception to the rule of avoiding contact with the Little People. Cherokee healers and spiritual leaders, sometimes called medicine men, would gather in the caves to meet with the Little People and learn their secrets. For seven days and nights they would tell stories around the campfire. Each night they would sing and dance together. During that time each medicine man would be given a secret by the Little People, and the medicine man would return the secret he had been given at the last gathering.

CHAPTER 4

Myth in Daily Life

Native Americans' spiritual beliefs were a basic and essential part of their lives. "Mythology, religion, history, and ritual were not separate things for Native American peoples. They were strands woven together in the various tales and stories that defined peoples' identity and gave order and meaning to their lives."[15] Their worldview was that everything on Earth was animated by spirit, and so their daily lives were influenced by the spirit world. Because unpleasant things could happen if someone offended a spirit, people were careful to give the proper respect to the spirit world in everything they did. The mythologies of the cultures acted as guides that explained how people should live their daily lives and often warned about what not to do. An important element of the daily life of First Peoples was the counseling or intercession of a medicine man or medicine woman.

The Role of the Medicine Man

According to a Cherokee myth, Ocasta, or Stonecoat, was a powerful supernatural being. He was named for the coat he wore, which was made of slivers of flint, a quartz rock used to make sparks. Ocasta was not all good or all bad, but

A Native American medicine man tends to a patient. The role of the medicine man varied among tribes, but he typically served as a healer, spiritual guide, rainmaker, and prophet.

he enjoyed causing trouble and was the creator of witches. He was killed by a group of angry village women. The men of the village burned the dying being, and as the flames claimed him Ocasta taught the men songs and dances for many things, including healing. Ocasta's great knowledge and power transferred to some of the men who became the first medicine men.

English-speaking people were the first to describe Native American healers as medicine men or women. In some cases they are called shamans. Although Native Americans feel that neither term properly describes the American Indian healer or spiritual leader, "medicine man" is typically used.

The responsibilities of the medicine man were slightly different for each culture, but in general they were the guardians of myth, important participants in ceremonies of birth, death, and others, as well as healers, spiritual guides, rainmakers, and even prophets. In some cases a medicine man communicated with a guardian spirit who might give him information or power. Because of this close association with spirits, in some tribes medicine men were feared and lived in isolation until they were needed. In contrast, several important chiefs were medicine men, including Sitting Bull (Lakota Sioux), Geronimo (Chiricahua Apache), and Cochise (Chiricahua Apache).

In many modern societies, when people become sick, a doctor treats the symptoms of the illness. Native American medicine men treated the whole person. They believed that illness resulted from disharmony with nature. Through ritual a medicine man used the forces of nature to restore harmony to the sufferer. Author Charles Alexander Eastman (Native American name Ohiyesa) explains, "The Sioux word for the healing art is wah-pee-yah, which literally means readjusting or making anew."[16] According to David Winston, a Cherokee medicine man and herbalist, "Cherokee medicine is based on connection—body, mind, spirit, family, community and God/Spirit. The Cherokee word for medicine, Nvowti, means power. Anything that has power—water, ceremony, songs, stories, herbs—is medicine."[17] Many myths supported that belief, and Native American mythologies are filled with stories of healing plants and ceremonies.

Arctic peoples used the term "Angakok" to describe their spiritual leader. The Angakok was similar to Asian shamans because he could enter a trance-like state and travel between the natural and supernatural worlds. He could communicate with Sedna, the goddess of the ocean, and some were said to journey under water to appease Sedna by combing her long, dark hair. The Angakok had a spirit guide that could

Working Together

The medicine people of the Karok were usually women. They were known as barking doctors and root doctors. The barking doctor determined the cause of a problem by squatting in front of the patient and barking at him or her. The root doctor used natural remedies to heal the ailment discovered by the barking doctor.

protect him and grant him powers such as great speed or the ability to fly. Like medicine men, the Angakok was a healer and could control the weather. He also performed ceremonies to ensure successful hunts.

Ceremony: The Blessingway and the White Deerskin Dance

In Native American cultures certain myths formed the basis of sacred rituals, including ceremonies in which participants acted out traditional sacred stories. Changing Woman was one of the most important figures in Navajo tradition, and her story is the basis for one of the most significant ceremonies of the Navajo, the Blessingway. Changing Woman represented the natural order and cycles of the universe: the cycle of the seasons and the stages of life from birth, maturity, old age, death, and rebirth. The story begins when people emerged from below onto the surface of Earth. When monsters attacked them, only First Man and First Woman survived. One day, First Man found a baby on a nearby mountain and showed her to the Holy People, the beings whose actions are told in stories and myths. The baby matured from infancy to her early teens in four days and so became known as Changing Woman. The Holy People blessed the girl and rinsed her hair with dew. They told her to run toward the dawn as far as she could see and then to return. She repeated this for four nights. From then on all young Navajo girls went through a similar ceremony when they reached their teens. The songs that were sung for Changing Woman as she ran are sung today for young girls at their own ceremonies.

Changing Woman eventually gave birth to two sons: Monster Slayer and Born for Water. Her sons also grew to boyhood in four days. In twelve days they were grown young men. Her sons rid the land of dangerous monsters and made it safe. Changing Woman created the Navajo People from skin rubbed off various parts of her body. The first four pairs of people created at that time were the ancestors of all the Navajo. When Changing Woman decided to teach the Blessingway ceremony to the two children of Rock Crystal

Talking God, the original Navajo saw it and so passed it down to their children. The purpose of the two-day ceremony is to ensure peace, harmony, protection, and a long and happy life. The Blessingway related the instructions Changing Woman gave to the Navajo people she created. It addresses many areas of life, such as coming of age, marriage, and the consecration of a home.

The walls of the traditional Navajo home, or hogan, were made of logs, bark, and packed earth according to directions in the Navajo creation story. It had a dome-shaped roof to represent Father Sky and a packed earth floor to represent Mother Earth. The door faced east to represent the world as described in the creation myth, and it had four posts to represent the four sacred mountains. The hogan is a sacred place for a Navajo family, and its proper construction honors their people and their land.

The Yurok of Northern California also performed a reenactment of their creation myth. Known as the White Deerskin Dance, it was meant to return the natural world to its

The Navajo built their hogans, a traditional dome-shaped home, according to the details of their creation myth.

stable and orderly state. "The ceremony is designed to correct temporary flaws in the relationship of the human community to the natural world and thus to enable the seasonal cycles to continue properly."[18] Seasonal cycles included the life cycle of the salmon, which was critically important to the well-being of the Yurok.

The dance, which lasted ten days or more, was related to the fishing season and the First Salmon Ceremony. The White Deerskin Dance was performed at the same time that a salmon dam, or weir, was built at the village of Kepel on the Klamath River. A weir was designed to slow the salmon and served as a platform that made it easier to catch the fish. People who helped to build the weir earned a place on it. The dam at Kepel took ten days to build, and there was a great deal of ritual and celebration associated with it.

No one could catch and eat a salmon until after the First Salmon Ceremony, in which a specially trained man called a formulist or ritualist approached the first netted salmon in the water and asked it if it was willing to be eaten. The salmon answered by floating in certain patterns. The fish was then killed and cooked and eaten in a particular manner. The ritual secured the success of the fishing season for the Yurok. If it had been properly performed, the people received permission from the spirit world to fish for salmon.

Hunting and Agriculture

The creation story of the Micmac people of the Northeast woodlands underlined the importance of the relationship between nature and the people. In the tale, the Sun was the creator and giver of life. A bolt of lightning from the Sun created man from a mound of sand. Next, man's grandmother was created. She taught the respectful way to hunt and explained that man had to ask an animal its permission to kill it. The hunter also had to give something back to thank the animal that had sacrificed itself. Dozens of Native American myths gave examples of how hunters should honor the animals they hunted by taking only what they needed and wasting nothing.

This myth, called Coyote and the Buffalo, from the Crow Nation of the Great Plains, even explains a technique for

Cornhusk Dolls

Native Americans of the Northeast woodlands have made cornhusk dolls for hundreds of years. When soaked the green husks are soft enough to shape and tie. The body is stuffed with leaves and the arms and legs may be rolled or braided from strips of husk. Corn silk serves as hair. Once they dry again the dolls are very sturdy. Sometimes the maker would draw a face on the doll, but usually the face was left blank. The Seneca people tell a story about why the cornhusk doll has no face. The creator made the first cornhusk doll and gave her a beautiful face. The doll traveled from village to village, making children happy everywhere she went. Many people told her how pretty she was and she began to think that her beauty was more important than her duty to entertain children. The doll would sit by streams and ponds admiring her reflection in the water, and she began to neglect the children. The creator warned her not to pay so much attention to how she looked, but the doll did not listen. To punish her the creator took away her face, and from then on cornhusk dolls usually had no facial features. Another reason to leave a doll faceless is to protect it from being possessed by an evil spirit that might enter through the eyes. In addition to their role as children's toys, some cornhusk dolls were used in healing ceremonies. For example, dolls made in a particular way were used to ward off the evil experienced in a nightmare.

Cornhusk dolls have been made by the tribes of the Northeast for centuries.

hunting buffalo. Old Man Coyote was walking across a small plateau when he spotted a large herd of buffalo. He wanted to make a meal of them, but he was alone and too small to capture one. He sat on the ground for a few minutes scanning the horizon and thinking. Then he saw the edge of the cliff in the distance and came up with a plan. Coyote approached the buffalo and told them that they were unlucky to have such bulky bodies with heavy heads, short legs, big bellies, and tiny eyes. One of the buffalo answered that the creator had made them that way, and they were just as good as Coyote. Old Man Coyote said they should prove that by running a race with him. He said when he gave the signal they would all close their eyes and see who could run the farthest without looking. The race began, and the buffalo thundered forward. When Coyote gave the signal they closed their eyes and did not see him stop, nor did they see the edge of the cliff. The herd tumbled one after another over the cliff, falling to their death below. Old Man Coyote feasted for a long time on their meat.

For hundreds of years Native Americans such as the Crow hunted buffalo on foot. Large groups of men gathered to herd the animals over cliffs called buffalo jumps to their deaths below. In one of his journals, Meriwether Lewis of the Lewis and Clark expedition explained how the buffalo were lured over the edge. He wrote that a swift young man in a buffalo skin robe would take a position between the herd and the cliff. At a signal, dozens of men would surround the herd on three sides and startle the buffalo. Lewis wrote, "The disguised Indian or decoy has taken care to place himself sufficiently near

Native American hunters drive a herd of buffalo off a cliff, a hunting technique explained by the Crow in the myth of Coyote and the Buffalo.

the buffalo to be noticed by them when they take to flight and running before them they follow him in full speed to the precipice; the Indian (decoy) in the mean time has taken care to secure himself in some cranny in the cliff . . . the part of the decoy I am informed is extremely dangerous."[19] At the base of the cliff the hunters could retrieve huge quantities of meat and hides that they could use, preserve, or trade.

Food and Farming

Many Native American mythologies include stories about how the people were to gather certain foods and the elements needed for cooking, such as oil and salt. The myth of the Three Sisters, which was widespread among Native American farming societies, explained the origin of three important crops and instructed that they should be grown together. One version is based on the Iroquois creation myth of Sky Woman. Sky Woman had fallen to Earth from a hole in the sky and had landed safely on an island on the back of a turtle. She had been about to have a child before she fell. Soon after she landed, she gave birth to a daughter. The daughter grew into a young beautiful young woman who died while giving birth to twin boys. Sky Woman buried her daughter and cried over the burial mound. Three sacred plants grew from the grave, the Three Sisters corn, beans, and squash. Each of the three crops were watched over by three sister spirits.

Corn, beans, and squash were the most important crops of many tribes throughout the Northeast and Southeast woodlands. To grow them farmers created mounds of soil in the fields. The Cherokee tilled each mound three times and buried some fish in the soil to add nutrients. Three seeds were traditionally planted in the same mound. The beans fixed nitrogen in the soil, making it more fertile. The tall corn plants supported the beans, and the wide squash leaves shaded the soil, keeping it cool and free of weeds and slowing the evaporation of water. One version or another of this

Chief of the Cherokee

Wilma Pearl Mankiller (1945–2010) was the principal chief of the Cherokee from 1985 to 1995. She was their first female chief of the twentieth century. She was *Ms.* magazine's Woman of the Year in 1987 and was inducted into the National Women's Hall of Fame in 1993.

Native American farmers harvest corn, an important crop that was first presented to the people, along with squash and beans, in the myth of the Three Sisters.

sophisticated, sustainable system provided a healthy diet to many different tribes in many regions for generations. The corn was boiled, roasted, made into cornmeal or flour for bread or cooked into mush. The husks were braided into mats, and the stalks were burned. Beans and squash could be eaten fresh or in stews. They could also be dried and stored for use in the winter, and anything left over might be given to tribal dogs.

Tribal Dogs

Before Europeans brought the horse to North America the dog was one of the most important domesticated animals in Native American daily life. Dogs carried packs and pulled sleds and heavy loads. They protected homes and livestock, helped to find people who were lost, and joined in hunting parties. The Blackfoot relied heavily on tribal dogs when moving their camps. The dogs carried provisions, tools, and utensils, and sometimes the strips used to build a family lodge. Dogs also hauled the travois, a type of sled that could hold bundles and sometimes babies. Some tribes revered the dog and included them in religious ceremonies. There are a variety of myths from many regions that explain how the relationship between human and canine came to be.

Over time many Native American myths have been lost. In some cases the origin of certain myths is uncertain. That is the case for this myth about the origin of the bond between humans and dogs. Shortly after the creator had finished crafting the earth and populating it with people and animals, the ground began to shake and a wide chasm began to form. The split separated First Man and First Woman from the rest of the animal kingdom. Dog sat at the edge watching the humans move away and seemed to be thinking. At last he backed up to get a running start and leaped across the divide. He caught the edge of the opposite side and barely hung on with his claws. First Man and First Woman reached down and lifted Dog up. He had risked his life to stay by the side of people, and from then on Dog's descendents remained at the side of humans.

In the mythology of the Ojibwa of the subarctic region there is a tale of how the dog came to live with humans. It began as two warriors paddled along the seacoast. When a storm blew in they became lost. Exhausted from battling the angry sea, they rested in their canoe until they felt it bump onto a beach. Cautiously, the men explored the area. It was not long before they found some huge footprints. They were terrified when a monstrous giant came through the trees and lumbered toward them, but he held out his massive hand in friendship and offered to take the men to his camp so that they could have a meal. The men agreed to go with the giant. When they reached his camp, something stirred in the woods and an evil Windigo leaped from the trees. Before the hungry cannibal monster could reach the men, the giant turned over a large bowl near the fire. Under

Native American Indian Dog

There are several types of American Indian dogs, but all are loyal and hard-working. The Native American Indian Dog (or NAID) of today looks much like those that lived in early Native American villages. It is a large, thick-coated dog that can weigh 80 pounds (36 kg) or more.

A family travels with the help of dogs that carry packs of their possessions. Dogs played a critical role in the daily life of Native Americans and are thus included in their mythology.

the bowl was a strange animal that the men had never seen before. It looked much like a wolf as it showed its sharp teeth. Growing bigger and bigger the animal attacked the Windigo and killed it. The strange animal shrunk back to its small size and crawled back under the bowl. The giant told the men that the animal was called Dog. He offered to give it to the warriors, and they happily accepted. When they walked back to the seashore Dog was with them. At the water's edge Dog grew again, and the giant put the two men onto its back, telling them to hold on very tightly. Dog ran into the sea and swam along the shore until the men recognized their home. Once on dry land Dog returned to its small size and joined the tribe as First Dog. Tales such as these were often preserved and shared by tribal storytellers.

Storytelling

According to a Seneca myth, a young boy who had been hunting birds stopped to rest next to a large stone that looked something like a human head. The youth was letting his thoughts drift when a voice suddenly declared that it was about to tell a story. The startled boy realized that the

Storytellers in Other Cultures

Native American storytellers use many techniques when they share tales with an audience, including singing and dancing. This is also true for the griot of West Africa. The griot is a human library who preserves the tribal history of his or her region through music, poetry, and storytelling. There was no written language in ancient Africa, so, like the myths of North America, the stories of West Africa have been kept alive through an oral tradition. For hundreds of years griots safeguarded the details of West African history and ancestry. Using drums, rattles, or a harplike instrument called a kora, a village storyteller would call to people to gather in the evening to hear tales about the history of the tribe, great leaders, battles, or even everyday life. The villagers might clap along as the griot told stories of mythological beings including gods, goddesses, heroes, and tricksters such as Anansi the Spider. The village griot was respected and in some cases even feared because of his or her tremendous body of knowledge. It was an inherited profession, passed on from one generation to the next, and if one village tried to take a storyteller from another, the result could be a serious conflict. The griot might know hundreds of stories, and it is said that when a griot dies, a library has burned to the ground.

Two griots from West Africa preserve their culture through storytelling.

voice belonged to the stone he was leaning against. It identified itself as Hahskwahot, the Great Stone. The stone asked for a gift in exchange for a story. The boy offered a bird, and the Great Stone told the tale of Sky Woman. That cold winter night the boy shared the story with his people, who were thrilled to hear it. The next day the boy returned to Hahskwahot and made another exchange. In this manner he heard dozens of stories by day and shared them around the campfires at night. At last Hahskwahot told the youth that he had given all of the stories he knew. He said that the boy should share the stories and learn new ones. "And wherever you go you will be welcomed and fed, as it is right to do to the storyteller. I have spoken."[20]

Many myths were recited during important rituals and ceremonies, but as in the tale of Hahskwahot, stories were

An elderly man tells a story to members of his tribe gathered around a campfire. Through storytelling, Native Americans have passed along not only their myths but their history, culture, and traditions.

often shared around a campfire. The Ojibwa thought that snakes and frogs were evil and might try to listen in. For that reason they believed that some myths could only be told on long winter nights so they would not be overheard by the snakes and frogs. As the Great Stone had said, the story-teller was traditionally fed and given gifts, such as tobacco, beads, or blankets for sharing. Some tribes even offered a well-known storyteller a valuable gift such as a horse.

Good storytellers were actors who used tone and gestures to add drama to a telling. Authors of the Indian Country website describe some of the typical storytelling techniques: "Some myths were long, often taking many hours to relate, and were often full of repetitious phrases that were well known to the listeners. It is not unusual for a story to come to an abrupt halt rather than a finished ending, occasionally with use of a phrase such as "That is as far as the story goes," or "That is the way they tell it."[21]

To Native Americans, myths were much more than just stories. They included valuable information about the tradi-tions, culture, and history of the people who honored them and so played an important role in their daily lives.

CHAPTER 5

The Survival of Myth

I n the Cheyenne myth of Arrow Boy, when Motzeyouf was an old man he told his people to "Beware the light-skinned strangers" who would "turn the whole world into stone."[22] In 1492 Christopher Columbus landed on the shores of an island in what is now the Bahamas and forever changed the course of North America. The interaction brought about many changes, but few had a positive effect on the mythologies of native North American cultures.

The introduction of the horse by the Spanish was one event that encouraged new stories to be told, such as those of Long Arrow and the Elk Dog. This Blackfoot legend explains that Long Arrow was an orphan boy adopted by the chief of his tribe. The chief told the boy about powerful spirit people who lived at the bottom of a lake near their village. The spirits raised strange animals called Elk Dogs that carried beings on their backs and did hard work such as pulling sleds. Every fourth generation a young man from the tribe dove into the lake to try to capture an Elk Dog, but none ever returned. Long Arrow begged his father to let him try to capture an Elk Dog and promised that he would succeed. Reluctantly the chief let him go. On his journey Long Arrow befriended a spirit boy who presented him to the Spirit Chief. Because the human boy showed great courage and respect, the Spirit

Chief rewarded Long Arrow with an Elk Dog to bring to his father. In time the people learned to use the strange animal that was, in fact, a horse.

Horses were once native to the North American continent, but they became extinct. Domestic horses returned with the Spanish conquistadors in the sixteenth century. Some escaped and others may have been set free, but they adapted well and formed large feral (wild) herds. The Blackfoot believed wild horses were gifts from a mythical figure named Old Man, a sometimes helpful trickster who was responsible for many elements of the world of the Blackfoot. Old Man had already given them elk, antelope, buffalo, and bighorn sheep, so they accepted the gift, calling the animal Elk Dog or Sky Dog. Some Native American cultures readily accepted the horse and became capable riders. The Nez Percé of the Great Plateau began to breed the horse and developed the Palouse or Appaloosa, one of the first true American breeds.

A Blackfoot warrior rides atop his horse in the 1830s. After horses were introduced to the Blackfoot, the tribe incorporated them into their mythology with a story about an animal called an Elk Dog.

The Appaloosa

Although the modern Appaloosa horse may have a solid coat color, it is best known for colorful, spotted coat patterns. A popular breed, it was named the official state horse of Idaho in 1975. It is used for show and western riding and several sports, including rodeo, jumping, and dressage.

Unlike the introduction of the horse, other changes brought about by the spread of European culture had devastating effects on North America's First Peoples and in turn, on their oral traditions. Native Americans lacked immunity to the diseases carried by Europeans. Millions became sick and died from measles, chicken pox, typhus, typhoid fever, dysentery, scarlet fever, diphtheria, and smallpox. Many oral myths died with them. Other changes altered the lifestyles of many tribes. Trade with the newcomers forever changed the traditional way of life for subarctic cultures. Nomadic hunters became trappers. They established villages near trading posts where they swapped the pelts of beaver and other small mammals for goods such as fabric, wool blankets, copper pots, and guns. In California the Spanish Mission system was designed to convert California tribes to Christianity, but the natives fell prey to disease, and their way of life was destroyed. As the United States grew and prospered, population pressures caused by new settlements, the culture of land ownership, and the discovery of gold all contributed to the movement and relocation of many tribes. In the Southeast woodlands, Cherokee, Creek, Seminole, and Choctaw nations were removed from their homelands and forced to travel by foot to the Indian Territory in what is now Oklahoma. Of the fifteen thousand relocated Cherokee, more than four thousand died during the journey from exposure, disease, and starvation.

As native people were relocated or lost to disease, the land itself was irreparably altered. Buffalo were systematically killed, and forests and prairies were cleared for settlement or farming. In the land where the Yurok once carefully managed the use of salmon, the forests fell to logging operations and roads and were cleared for railroad tracks. Streambeds became unpassable, and the special conditions that salmon needed to spawn were gradually destroyed so the fish disappeared. The destruction of the Great Basin's sacred piñon nut forests came in waves. Trees were toppled to obtain wood for mine construction and to build houses, furniture, and wagons. The building of the transcontinental railroad and the use of wood for fuel contributed to the deforestation of millions of acres of forest.

Between the years of 1790 and 1920 a policy was put in place to assimilate, or absorb, Native Americans into the general culture of the United States. It was based on the concept that if American Indians adopted the Euro-American ways they would fit more easily into society and be able to get a formal education and find work. In the late nineteenth and early twentieth centuries, the U.S. government made the practice of many traditional religious ceremonies illegal. Native American children were separated from their parents and required to attend boarding schools where they were forced to speak only English, cut their hair, wear European-style clothing, and attend church. Captain

A group of Chiracahua Apache students at the Carlisle Indian Industrial School pose in suits and dresses in 1886. Government programs forced many Native American children to attend boarding schools, where they were required to speak English and wear European-style clothing.

Richard C. Pratt, founder of the Carlisle Indian Industrial School in Pennsylvania, claimed that it was best to "kill the Indian, and save the man."[23]

Native American mythology was traditionally kept alive by communal and cultural practices, ceremony, ritual, and a deep connection with the environment outlined in the myths. Because of the systematic destruction of American Indian cultures, their mythologies nearly disappeared, which would have been a tragic loss on many levels. Authors David Leeming and Jake Page describe the importance of mythology to its culture: "A myth is a reflection of a culture's soul, its inner sense of itself."[24] Fortunately Native Americans found ways to preserve and protect their stories, and some were recorded by early missionaries and explorers.

The Survival of Myth

The first Europeans to record the myths of North America were Jesuit missionaries. In the seventeenth century they established a series of missions in the northeastern regions. For the time period, their approach was marginally respectful of the Native Americans' traditions and customs. Many of the missionaries studied the native languages and created valuable dictionaries.

Henry Rowe Schoolcraft was responsible for the preservation of some myths. He was a nineteenth century explorer and geologist who discovered the source of the Mississippi River. Schoolcraft's wife, Jane, was part Ojibwa and taught him the language and lore of her people. As an agent of the U.S. government, he worked to settle a dispute between the Ojibwa and Dakota people and was later appointed superintendent of Indian Affairs in the Northern Department. During the course of his time in the northeast and Great Lakes regions Schoolcraft compiled an important collection of Native American stories and legends.

Between the 1880s and the 1930s, anthropologists, historians, and linguists interviewed Native Americans and recorded their myths. The stories, however, were "recorded by non-Natives and translated into English; because the translation process involves some interpretation, it does not result in a perfect replica of the original source,"[25] according

Totem Poles

The totem poles of the Pacific Northwest coast are highly valued works of art. They were usually carved from the trunks of large red cedar trees up to 40 feet (12m) high. Some were painted and others were not. The word "totem" is from the Ojibwa term *odoodem*, meaning kinship group, and many totem poles were designed to show the lineage of a particular clan and the link to their spirit ancestors. Totem poles were often raised to show the rights a person had acquired over their lifetime, to celebrate the generosity of the host of a potlatch ceremony in which ceremonial gifts were given to attendees, or to document an encounter with a supernatural being. They also depicted mythological beings or illustrated stories, legends, or important events. Some carvings were even meant to be playful, with upside-down figures or funny images. The order of the carvings on the pole was not the most important consideration. Significant images could be at the top or at the base of the finished piece. In fact, because the lower portion of the pole was the easiest to view, greater care was often given to the carving of the images at the center. Early European missionaries mistakenly thought that the pillars were religious objects and insisted that they be burned, but the poles were never used as objects of worship or to ward off evil spirits. Still, it is considered bad luck to kick a totem pole. Although red cedar resisted decay, few totem poles of today are more than one hundred years old. The tallest existing pole carved by Native Americans is in Kake, Alaska, It was carved by the Chilkats in 1967 to honor Alaska's centennial and is an astonishing 132 feet (40m) tall.

A totem pole that stands near Ketchikan, Alaska, includes carvings of faces and animals.

to authors of the *Handbook of Native American Mythology*. The libraries of several modern colleges and universities have collections of myths, some in native languages, that were retrieved from government documents and published in academic journals. In the twentieth century tribal governments began to collect the myths of their people that had been hidden and protected. They have also taken steps toward reclaiming sacred sites.

Native American myths are taking their place in the study of world mythology, and people of many cultures are exploring native traditions, particularly those that teach how to live in harmony with nature. Author Arthur Versluis notes that "there is evidence that many Americans and European-Americans are willing, indeed eager, to learn about traditional tribal spirituality."[26] Still, American Indians point out that native heritage is passed through bloodlines, not by practicing their ceremonies and traditions.

Mythology and Native American Art, Literature, and Film

As native traditions become more familiar, people of all cultures are studying and discovering American Indian fine art, crafts, and literature, which are often inspired by myths. The art and craft forms include beadwork, weaving, sculptures, and more. Sandpainting was a critical element of Navajo healing ceremonies. A traditional sandpainting was not meant to be permanent. The act of creation was more important than preserving the work. While chanting, a medicine man created the work on the ground by trickling colored sands through his fingers in intricate images. Such images may be of the Holy People of myth. When the work was complete a patient sat on the painting as the healer chanted. If done correctly, the Holy People would absorb the illness. The sandpainting itself would be completely destroyed at the end of the ceremony. Outsiders were not allowed to witness the ritual, and the sacred paintings were not allowed to be photographed. In the 1940s some medicine men agreed to create permanent sandpaintings that could be displayed publicly. To protect their tradition, errors were introduced into the imitations.

For example, colors were reversed or the designs were altered. The permanent sandpaintings sold in shops today are commercially produced and also contain errors.

A Navajo artist creates a sandpainting. Traditionally used in healing ceremonies, the designs are considered sacred.

One of the oldest native crafts is basket weaving. Different tribes used different materials, techniques, and patterns. The materials depended on what was available in the environment. Baskets of the Southwest were often made from coiled sumac or willow wood. The eastern regions used braided sweetgrass or bundled pine needles. The Oneida people often exchanged baskets for the telling of a legend or myth. In the subarctic they used birch bark, and Northwest coastal tribes used cedar. The coastal Salish people tell a story of a

Native American Musicians

There are many famous Native American traditional musicians, but several are award-winning artists in other musical styles. Robbie Robertson (1943–), born in Canada to a Jewish father and a Mohawk mother, is a successful rock musician. He was a singer and songwriter in an acclaimed group of the 1960s and 1970s called The Band. Their hit songs included "I Shall Be Released" (1967) written by Bob Dylan and "The Weight" (1968). Robertson was ranked seventy-eighth in *Rolling Stone* magazine's list of the 100 Greatest Guitarists of All Time. Buffy Sainte-Marie (1941–) is a Canadian folksinger and songwriter. A descendant of the Cree, she is best known for her antiwar song "Universal Soldier" (1964) and for her Academy Award–winning song "Up Where We Belong" (1982). Steven Tyler is an American musician and songwriter and the lead singer of the Boston-based rock band Aerosmith.

The group has numerous multiplatinum records to their credit, and their lengthy list of hits includes "Walk This Way" (1975) and "Dream On" (1973). Tyler's Cherokee heritage is from his mother's side of his family.

Buffy Sainte-Marie is an award-winning Canadian folksinger and songwriter of Cree heritage.

man who was always willing to help those in need. When he died, the Great Spirit honored the kind man by causing a great red cedar tree to grow from the grave so that he could continue to give. The roots of the red cedar are traditionally used for baskets.

American Indian pottery traditions were diverse. The forms, colors, and designs from each region were quite distinct, but most made coil and pinch pots by hand. The spiritual nature of pottery making is described by author and art therapy expert Elizabeth Warson:

> When the Indian potter collects clay, she asks the consent of the river-bed and sings its praises for having made something as beautiful as clay. When she fires her pottery she offers songs to the fire so it will not discolour or burst her wares. And, finally, when she paints her pottery, she imprints it with the images that give it life and power—because for an Indian, pottery is something significant, not just a utility but a "being" for which there is as much of a natural order as there is for persons or foxes or trees.[27]

The connection between art and myth is clear in southwestern pottery because potters often decorated their creations with spirits such as the Navajo Yeii, an intermediary between man and the creator, and Kokopelli, a common fertility symbol throughout the Southwest. Native American potters, such as Iris Nampeyo of the Hopi tribe, have gained wide recognition.

Literature

Zitkala Sa (1876–1938), a Yankton Sioux, was a celebrated musician and author. Born Gertrude Simmons, she was separated from her family at age eight and was raised in the boarding school system. As a young adult at the beginning of the twentieth century, Simmons began to write and publish stories under the name of Zitkala Sa, or Red Bird. Because of her talent Zitkala Sa gained tremendous recognition from mainstream society. Her stories were published in prestigious magazines such as *Atlantic Monthly* and *Harper's Monthly*. Her first book, *Old Indian Legends*, is a collection of Native American myths and folktales.

More recently, authors such as Leslie Marmon Silko (1948–) have blended myth and tradition into contemporary stories. In her 1986 book *Ceremony* Silko tells the tale of a group of American Indian World War II veterans. With the help of a medicine man, the main character, Tayo, discovers his connection to the land and comes to understand the need to create ceremonies. Silko revealed "a world that arises out of an oral, not written, tradition—one in which signs and omens, and various non-verbal perceptions, feelings, intuitions and sensations carry a weight and meaning unknown to Euro-centric society,"[28] says reviewer Ken Lopez.

Joseph Bruchac (1942–) is a prolific writer who has authored more than fifty books for adults and children. A native Abenaki, Bruchac uses his knowledge of Native American myth and storytelling to spin some frightening tales. *The Dark Pond* is the story of a part-Shawnee boy named Armin who is able to communicate with animals. The boy learns about a pond where animals enter but do not leave, and he must find the secret of what the Iroquois and Abenaki say is the lair of underwater monsters. Bruchac's books *Skeleton Man* and *Return of Skeleton Man* also feature a terrifying monster that threatens the family of Molly, a part-Mohawk girl. Native American mythological characters and legends regularly appear in horror tales. *The Wendigo* is the title of a novella by master horror writer Algernon Blackwood. The cannibal monster of the subarctic tribes also appears in the twenty-fifth anniversary edition of *Scary Stories to Tell in the Dark* by Alvin Schwartz.

Poet, filmmaker, and author Sherman Alexie (1966–) is a native Spokane of the Northwest coastal region. He has won many awards for his work, including the California Young Reader medal and the National Book Award for his semiautobiographical young adult novel *The Absolutely True Diary of a Part-Time Indian*. Several of his works address the importance of the storyteller in Native American culture. The myths of the Northwest coastal tribes are also featured in the blockbuster series Twilight by Stephenie Meyer. One of the main characters is a shape-shifter known in European tradition as a werewolf. The Twilight series has also been produced as successful films.

Films about Native Americans have been popular since the industry began. At first, American Indian characters were often negative stereotypes, and their traditions were inaccurately portrayed. A more recent film that gained critical acclaim and box office success was *Dances with Wolves* (1990). In the movie

Lieutenant John Dunbar, played by actor Kevin Costner, is a Civil War hero assigned to an outpost on the western frontier. He is accepted into a local tribe and learns to respect the culture and wisdom of the native people. Another recent film, *Indian in the Cupboard* (1995), features a nine-year-old white boy named Omri, played by Hal Scardino. On his birthday Omri receives, among other gifts, an old cupboard with a lock but no key. With the help of his mother he finds a key that fits and tests it by locking a plastic Indian figure in the cupboard. When he opens it again the figure is alive. Omri learns that Little Bear is an Iroquois. The more Omri discovers about the true ways of Little Bear's people the more he comes to love and admire his friend. As it is with literature, many horror films and television shows feature the monsters of American Indian myth, beginning with the silent film *The Lure of the Windigo* (1914). Popular television series such as *The X-Files*, *Charmed*, and *Supernatural* have also featured the Windigo.

In the twenty-first century a growing number of independent films by Native American directors, producers, writers, actors, and musicians are available. The films and their creators are showcased at festivals such as the Native American Film and Video Festival hosted each spring in New York by the Film and Video Center of the National Museum of the American Indian; the Red Fork Native American Film Festival in Oklahoma; and the Red Nation Film Festival held in Los Angeles in the fall. The festivals are helping to promote the filmmakers of the future.

The Native American Future

In an interesting Sioux story, the future of the world depends on an old black dog. He lives in a cave where the prairie and the badlands meet on the Great Plains. There, an old woman has been sitting in front of a fire for one thousand years decorating a strip for a buffalo robe. She is carefully threading it with colored porcupine quills. The dog sits beside her. Behind her is a pot of soup that has been bubbling for one thousand years. When the woman finishes decorating the strip the world will end, but every time she turns around to stir her soup, the dog pulls the porcupine quills out.

To the Cheyenne the fate of the world rests with a great white Grandfather Beaver. It is gnawing at the pole that holds up Earth. When it finally bites through and the pole topples, Earth will end. Storytellers claim he is already halfway through, and he chews faster when he is angry. That is why the Cheyenne do not eat beaver meat or wear its skins. They do not want to make Grandfather Beaver angry.

Prophetic vision is one aspect of some American Indian spiritual beliefs. Seeds for the myths and legends of the future may be planted in Native American prophecies. Some Hopi foretell a coming time called the Great Purification. A twenty-foot-high sandstone formation near Hotevilla in Navajo County, Arizona, shows the two paths that people might take at that time. It is covered with ancient carvings called petroglyphs. Although this formation was unguarded for hundreds of years, it is now protected by Hopi elders. The main carving is a figure representing the Earth guardian, Maasau. Two lines extend away from the figure. On the upper line are images of humans that appear to be slowly breaking apart. Beyond that the line seems to disintegrate. The people on the top line are greedy for material things that are not essential to unity and harmony. The lower line shows people who are in harmony with nature planting corn. At one point there is a line, or bridge, connecting the two lines. That is the time of Great Purification when people have a final chance to change. Once the bridge is passed or crossed there is no return.

On December 10, 1992, Thomas Banyacya, a Hopi elder, addressed the United Nations as part of an event to note the Year of Indigenous Peoples. He was the final speaker, and he mentioned an ancient prophecy that said some day world leaders would gather in a Great House of Mica to solve the world's problems without war. The United Nations building is all glass, and it is shiny in the sun like mica. Mr. Banyacya noted that the world was experiencing an increase in powerful storms, floods, earthquakes, and droughts, and

The Eagle Has Landed

According to ancient Hopi prophecy, "The truth of the Sacred Ways shall be revealed when the Eagle lands on the moon." On July 20, 1969, astronauts from NASA's Apollo 11 spaceflight landed on the moon in the lunar module named *Eagle*. Many believe that the prophecy was fulfilled when the astronauts reported, "The Eagle has landed."

Adishakti.org. "The Eagle Has Landed." www.adishakti.org/prophecies/25_white_buffalo_calf_woman_has_returned.htm.

animals and forests were disappearing in great numbers. He said it was time to make a decision, and it was time for indigenous cultures to return to their traditions. Thomas Banyacya passed away in 1999, but other elders have continued to speak his message, hoping that, as Larry Merculieff, a respected Aleut community advocate said in a speech given to Aleut elders, "the wisdom of how to work with Mother Earth will all be restored."[29]

NOTES

Introduction: The Nature of Myth

1. Dawn E. Bastian and Judy K. Mitchell. *Handbook of Native American Mythology.* New York: Oxford University Press, 2008, p. 1.
2. Mircea Eliade, *Myth and Reality.* Trans. Willard R. Trask. New York: Harper & Row, 1963. Quoted in M. Joseph, *In Search of Cupid and Psyche: Myth and Legend in Children's Literature.* Reprinted at The Structure of Myths website. Rutgers School of Communication and Information. http://comminfo.rutgers.edu/~mjoseph/eliade.html.
3. Bronislaw Malinowski. *Myth in Primitive Psychology.* New York: W.W. Norton, 1926. Reprinted in Bronislaw Malinowski. *Magic, Science and Religion.* Garden City, NY: Doubleday Anchor Books, 1955, p. 101.

Chapter 1: The First Peoples of North America

4. James Houston. "Inuit Myth and Legend." In *The Canadian Encyclopedia.* Historica Foundation, 2011. www.thecanadianencyclopedia.com/index.cfm?PgNm=TCE&Params=a1ARTA0004043.
5. Katherine Kirkpatrick. *Coyote and the Monster: A Creation Story.* katherinekirkpatrick.com. www.katherinekirkpatrick.com/coy_mons.html.

Chapter 2: The Universal Myths

6. Native Net. Native American Mythology. www.native-net.org/na/native-american-mythology.html.
7. Milwaukee Public Museum. "Oral Tradition." Indian Country. www.mpm.edu/wirp/icw-14.html.
8. Kurt Hübner. *Critique of Scientific Reason.* Trans. Paul R. Dixon. Chicago: University of Chicago Press, 1988, p. 271.
9. Sophia Blanche Lyon Fahs and Patricia Hoertdoerfer. *Long Ago and Many Lands: Stories for Children Told Anew.* Boston: Skinner House, 1995, p. 118.
10. Fred Ramen. *Native American Mythology.* New York: Rosen, 2008, p. 53.

11. Ramen. *Native American Mythology*, p. 53.

Chapter 3: Deities and Spirits

12. David Leeming and Jake Page. *The Mythology of Native North America*. Norman: University of Oklahoma Press, 1998, p. 71.
13. *Myth Encyclopedia*. "Spider Woman." www.mythencyclopedia.com/Sp -Tl/Spider-Woman.html.
14. Mary C. Churchill. "Encyclopedia of Religion." Vol. 14. 2nd ed. *Encyclopedia of Religion*. Ed. Lindsay Jones. Detroit: Macmillan Reference USA, 2005, pp. 9725–9726.

Chapter 4: Myth in Daily Life

15. *Myth Encyclopedia*. "Spider Woman." www.mythencyclopedia.com /Mi-Ni/Native-American-Mythology .html.
16. Charles Alexander Eastman (Ohiyesa). *The Soul of the Indian: An Interpretation*. Lincoln: University of Nebraska Press, 1911. www.guten berg.org/catalog/world/readfile?fk _files=1442104&pageno=1.
17. Quoted in Phyllis D. Light. "What the Medicine Men Knew." Overall Well-Being. Edible Nature. www .ediblenature.com/healthlibrary /What_The_Medicine_Men_Knew .htm.
18. American Indians Ready Reference. "White Deerskin Dance." Enotes .com, 2011. www.enotes.com/salem-history/white-deerskin-dance.
19. Meriwether Lewis and William Clark. *The Journals of Lewis And Clark*. Whitefish, MT: Kessinger, 2004, p. 111.
20. Ramen. *Native American Mythology*, p. 5.
21. Milwaukee Public Museum. "Oral Tradition."

Chapter 5: The Survival of Myth

22. Ramen. *Native American Mythology*, p. 53.
23. Richard Pratt. "Kill the Indian Save the Man." In *Official Report of the Nineteenth Annual Conference of Charities and Correction* (1892), pp. 46–59. Reprinted in Richard H. Pratt. "The Advantages of Mingling Indians with Whites." In *Americanizing the American Indians: Writings by the "Friends of the Indian," 1880–1900*. Cambridge, MA: Harvard University Press, 1973, pp. 260–271. http://socrates.bmcc .cuny.edu/bfriedheim/pratt.htm.
24. Leeming and Page. *The Mythology of Native North America*, p. 73.
25. Bastian and Mitchell. *Handbook of Native American Mythology*, p. 27.
26. Arthur Versluis. *Native American Traditions*. Salisbury, UK: Element, 1994, p. 8.
27. Elizabeth Warson. "From Foster-care to Indian Boarding School: Empowering Native Youth." In *Cre-

ative Arts Therapies Approaches in Adoption and Foster Care: Contemporary Strategies for Working with Individuals and Families. Edited by Donna J. Betts. Springfield, IL: Charles C. Thomas, 2003, p. 136.

28. Ken Lopez. "American Indian Authors and Literature." *IOBA Standard* vol. 3, no. 2 (May 2002). www.ioba.org/newsletter/archive/v7/KenLopezArticle.html.

29. Quoted in Larry Merculieff. "Let Goodness Take Its Place." Reprinted in "A Message to My People, Healing: An Alaskan Prophecy." Viewzone.com. http://viewzone2.com/alaskanx.html.

archaeologist: A scientist who studies the physical remains of ancient cultures.

confederation: A group of loosely allied states or groups.

conquistadors: Sixteenth-century Spanish soldiers.

consecration: A blessing or dedication.

indigenous: Native or original.

kayak: A light-framed, watertight, skin-covered canoe.

Lewis and Clark expedition: The first U.S. expedition to the Pacific Coast (1804–1806).

medicine bundle: A bag containing items of personal or religious significance.

migration: Movement of a group from one place to another.

nomadic: Of people who travel from place to place.

primordial: Primitive or prehistoric.

sweetgrass: A fragrant plant.

tepee: A portable dwelling for certain Native American people.

totem poles: A post carved and painted with animals, figures, or mythic beings.

travois: A frame slung between trailing poles and pulled by a dog or horse.

tubers: Underground starchy root of a plant such as a potato.

tundra: A treeless area of the Arctic with permanently frozen subsoil.

Books

James Bruchac and Joseph Bruchac. *The Girl Who Helped Thunder, and Other Native American Folktales.* Folktales of the World. New York: Sterling, 2008. An anthology of Native American tales. Every story begins with background information about the tribe of origin.

David Leeming and Jake Page. *The Mythology of Native North America.* Norman: University of Oklahoma Press, 1998. An extensive collection of myths.

Fred Ramen. *Mythology Around the World: Native American Mythology.* New York: Rosen, 2008. An overview of creation, animal, trickster, and hero myths.

Suzanne M. Williams. *The Inuit.* Danbury, CT: Franklin Watts, 2003. *The Inuit* explores history, traditions, legends, and today's Inuit people. The author worked with many Inuit people to produce the book.

Suzanne Morgan Williams. *The Cherokee.* Chicago: Heinemann Raintree, 2003. A book in the Native American Series, developed in conjunction with tribal people and highlighting the history, traditions, and modern life of native peoples. Other titles in the series include *The Tlingit, The Powhatan, The Chinook, The Ojibwe, The Iroquois, The Seminole, The Lakota,* and more.

Zitkala-Sa. *Iktomi and the Ducks, and Other Sioux Stories.* Lincoln: University of Nebraska Press/Bison Books, 2004. Fourteen stories collected and told by a renowned Native American author.

Websites

Access Genealogy (www.accessgenealogy.com/native). A site that contains extensive lists of tribal information, Native American records and rolls, as well as articles.

National Museum of the American Indian (www.nmai.si.edu). A Smithsonian museum site. Information on history, geography, and art. The collections include all major cultural areas of North America, all tribes of the United States, and many of Canada.

Native American Nations (www.nanations.com/linguistic_families.htm). A wonderful site filled with information on myths and legends as well as tribal information organized according to linguistic families.

Native Languages of the Americas (http://www.native-languages.org/home.htm). Information on dozens of Native American tribes, language, art, and myth.

Phoebe A. Hearst Museum of Anthropology (http://hearstmuseum.berkeley.edu/outreach/pdfs/teaching_kit.pdf). A teaching kit on California Indians with activities, photographs, glossary, and recipes.

The Yukon Beringia Interpretive Centre (www.beringia.com/education/index.html). A site for exploring the Yukon's recent prehistory. It includes information on First Peoples, activities, and current research.

INDEX

W

Washo Indians, 22

Wendigo. *See* Windigo

The Wendigo (Blackwood), 86

White Buffalo Women (Lakota myth),
    51–53

White Deerskin Dance (Yurok), 65–66

Windigo, 16, 71, 72, 88

Winnebago Indians, 25

Winston, David, 63

Wintun Indians, 34–35

World parent myths, 47–49

Y

Yakima Indians, 20, 22

Yggdrasil (World Tree), 34

Yundi Tsundi (Little People), 58

Yupik tribes, 14

Yurok Indians, 19
    creation myth of, 65–66

Z

Zitkala Sa (Gertrude Simmons),
    85

PICTURE CREDITS

Q.L. Pearce has written more than one hundred books for children and more than thirty classroom workbooks and teacher manuals on the topics of reading, science, math, and values. Pearce has written science-related articles for magazines; regularly gives presentations at schools, bookstores, and libraries; and is a frequent contributor to the educational program of the Los Angeles County Fair. She is an assistant regional adviser for the Society of Children's Book Writers and Illustrators.

Per RFP 03764 Follett School Solutions guarantees
hardcover bindings through SY 2024-2025
877.899.8550 or customerservice@follett.com